THE GREAT ONE

THE GREAT ONE

The Life and Times of
Wayne Gretzky

ANDREW PODNIEKS

TRIUMPH
BOOKS

This book is available in quantity at special discounts for your group or organization. For more information, contact:
Triumph Books
601 South LaSalle Street
Suite 500
Chicago, Illinois 60605
(312) 939-3330
Fax (312) 663-3557

Jacket photographs by Bruce Bennett Studios
Jacket and text design by Andrew Smith Graphics, Inc.
Printed and bound in the USA

ISBN 1-57243-352-3

TRIUMPH BOOKS
Distributed in the United States by Truimph Books
601 South LaSalle Street, Suite 500
Chicago, Illinois 60605
(312) 939-3330

Published by arrangement with
Doubleday Canada,
a division of Random House of Canada Ltd.
105 Bond Street
Toronto, Ontario
M5B 1Y3

RRD   10   9   8   7   6   5   4   3   2   1

CONTENTS

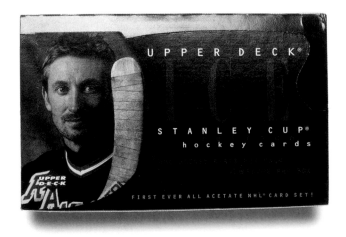

INTRODUCTION

I WAS NEVER A FAN OF THE OILERS in the eighties when they were at the height of their Stanley Cup powers. It looked so easy for them, this team that was born mostly out of view in the WHA, then burst into the NHL and won games by baseball and football scores of 10-8 or 8-7. They controlled the scoreboard, scored at will, and never, ever let up. It was that ruthlessness, if anything, that I admired without altogether cheering.

Gretzky and the Oilers never reacted to the game — they *anticipated* play. They knew what would happen next not as it was happening, but *before* it happened. Gretzky always broke out of his own zone really early—in shinny terms he'd be called a goal suck — while the other team still had the puck. But he recognized that in the next second his own player would get possession, he knew that his man would be looking for the fast break, and he knew that the pass would get to open ice if he were there for it.

The Oiler defencemen rarely hammered the puck inconsequentially off the glass and out to centre ice, not even short-handed. They seldom froze the puck in the corners or iced the puck (unless it was an errant breakaway pass). Everything they did was about moving towards the other goal as quickly as possible. Transition, speed, puck movement. Box formation, dump and chase, matching lines, all formal strategy, was old-style hockey.

Like so many others, I wondered why the opposition didn't hit Gretzky more often the way Bill McCreary had when he was called up briefly by the Leafs in 1981. Gretzky would slip in over the blueline at full speed, but he'd never go to the outside or try to muscle his way into the slot. Instead, he'd cut across the centre or curl back towards the line, but he always seemed to create more open ice and end up closer to the net! And if he were trapped, a short perfect pass to an open teammate would result in a great scoring chance.

The Gretzky I cherished was the one who always said yes to Canada. He played with a pride and dignity that every hockey player should aspire to when he puts on his national sweater. He recognized the honour involved in international competition, never presumed to be above his country's endeavours, and represented Canada with passion and, yes, success.

I was surprisingly sad the weekend of Gretzky's final games, in Ottawa and New York. The only other time I felt such admiration for someone was when Bobby Orr retired, though for different reasons. When Orr left the game, he did so because his ravaged knees prevented him from even skating. He gave the game everything he had. When Gretzky was young, I remember him saying he wasn't going to play for very long, maybe to 30, because he wanted to leave in good health. I knew then that he was lying to himself, that those were the selfish words of youth. When you can do something as well as he can, you don't stop until something tells you that tomorrow you won't be able to do what you did yesterday. As he had done throughout his career, he left the game at exactly the right moment. His greatest pass of all might have been knowing exactly when to give the torch to Kariya, Lindros, Jagr, and Forsberg.

Some of Gretzky's greatest moments have now, with time and their exceptionality, become part of the game's lexicon, its history, its glory: the 50th goal in his 39th game before a frenzied Edmonton crowd; his overtime short-handed goal against the Flames. There was the preposterous night the Leafs beat Edmonton 11-9 at Maple Leaf Gardens. Each time Gretzky played in Toronto he'd slaughter the home team, playing with a pride and passion that was the envy of every Leaf fan.

He scored so many slapshot goals, yet no one gave him credit for his shot, both its speed and its pinpoint accuracy. His second-to-last playoff hat trick, against Vanbiesbrouck and the Panthers, was capped by a shot he blew over Beezer's glove, his third goal in a span of just over six minutes. I'll always remember with jealousy the Stanley Cups he won in Edmonton, the first of which he was most proud, the last followed by the Oilers sitting for a team photo at centre ice. And, of course, there was his utter dejection on the bench after Canada lost the shoot-out he didn't participate in against Hasek in Nagano.

It's funny how times change. It was easy to hate the Oilers back then. They were so good and won at will, and the end seemed nowhere in sight. Now I cheer madly for them, a franchise that all of a sudden exists from year to year, removed from those Cups not just by talent but by the ugly dollar, the horror of the "small market" label, a bloated league that this year or next might not have room for one of Canada's most important hockey cities.

There are two moments — one on ice, the other off — that will always stay with me when I think of Gretzky. Off ice, on the day of his press conference in New York, he answered all the questions. Then, from the back of the room, Paul Romanuk and Bob McKenzie of TSN started a brief on-air summary of events, when, from out of nowhere, Gretzky materialized. He put his arms around their shoulders and said, "Got a few minutes?" then promptly talked to the two stunned men casually about what he had moments earlier formalized.

On ice, nothing compares to his drop pass to Lemieux that won the '87 Canada Cup. To a new generation of hockey fans, that was the closest thing we're likely to get to Henderson's goal for a long, long time to come.

ANDREW PODNIEKS

ONE

IN THE BEGINNING

ON THE DAY WAYNE DOUGLAS GRETZKY WAS BORN, January 26, 1961, Gordon Howe scored a goal at the Detroit Olympia to help give the Wings a 2-2 tie with the Blackhawks. The first child of Walter and Phyllis, Wayne weighed six pounds, eight ounces, about 170 below his playing weight when he entered the NHL as a spindly teenager some 18 years later. The story of how Wayne got from his tiny crib in Brantford, Ontario to his first backyard rink to playing with and against Howe in the NHL is one that transformed both the hockey world and the cultural landscape of Canadian society.

By the time Wayne was three his father had built a rink in the family's backyard on Varadi Avenue, not because he wanted a private training facility for his infant son but so that he could keep an eye on the youngster from the warmth of the family kitchen. "It was for self-preservation," he confessed. "I got sick of taking him to the park and sitting there for hours freezing to death."

Wayne spent untold hours on his little frozen lake, dubbed Wally's Coliseum, skating forward and backward, circling and pirouetting around Javex containers, shooting, deking, falling down and getting up smiling and laughing. When he was tired, he came in for dinner and went to bed after a short nightcap of one-on-himself shinny. Wayne's adult recollections of those early days pay due respect to his father: "He drove me and he didn't drive me," he said. "I used to go out after school for an hour and a half, and then I'd come in to eat dinner and when it came time to go out

again I'd be sitting there and he'd say, 'You didn't do any shooting or practising.' And I'd say, 'I didn't feel like it.' And he'd say, 'Well, someday you may have to get up at six-thirty and go to work from seven to five and you'd better feel like it.' Little things like that would give me the motivation. He never had to say, 'You turkey; you weren't out there shooting.' My dad was very smart."

His private arena was built for four winters. But while Wayne was becoming a superb skater, he couldn't play in a league until he was ten. Those were the rules. His dad took him to try out for the local Nadrofsky Steelers anyway, Wayne was six years old, all the other boys ten. At that age, of course, size and weight differences were significant, and he was so much smaller than his teammates that his #11 jersey practically touched the ice and interfered with his shooting. His dad tucked the back right side in, and in it stayed for good.

Wayne made the Steelers on the strength of his stick-handling; no one could get the puck from him when he had it. But as the season went on, parents lambasted Walter for sending this scrawny, under-sized kid out against much better young boys. Their evidence at season's end lay in the fact that Wayne had scored just one goal. The team trainer, though, Bob Phillips, actually gave Wayne that puck as a keepsake, a remarkably prescient gesture given this was 1968 (before collectibles were next to Godliness) and the recipient had just turned seven.

The next year — same league, same team — Gretzky scored 27 goals and received his first honour, the Wally Bauer Trophy as the most improved Novice all-star. The year after, he scored 104 goals, and now parents, in a fit of pique, were saying the season was a fluke; he'd never do *that* again. In fact, not only did he do that again,

he did it in *half* a season, finishing with 196 goals over the whole year. Now he was Brantford minor-league famous, and his father gave him the option of staying in Novice (under-10) one more year, or moving up to Peewee. He chose the former, and in his last year with Nadrofsky (1971–72) he scored 378 goals in 85 games, a preposterous number that no one could have predicted even as a silly joke at the beginning of the year.

It was October 28, 1971 that the first story on Wayne appeared in a major paper, *The Telegram*. In Grade 5 at Greenbrier Public School, the ten-year old avowed his love for his idol: "Gordie Howe is my kind of player. He had so many tricks around the net, no wonder he scored so many goals. I'd like to be just like him."

The idyllic image of a Wunderkind who grows up without worry in a small town is as much myth based on the fame that player ultimately achieves as it is on the daily

DURING THE 1973–74 SEASON, the Toronto Toros of the WHA played their home games at Varsity Arena. During the year, they had special CHUM Shootout contests (sponsored by the radio station of that name) wherein four local-area hockey players would take a penalty shot on a Toros goalie during the second intermission. One night, Wayne Gretzky (wearing his White Tornado gloves, far right) took part with John Rea (both gloves on his stick) and two other unidentified players. Les Binkley was the Toros goaler (notice his mask tucked into the top of his right pad) and he stopped all four shooters. After missing, Gretzky slammed his stick into the ice. "I could tell even then that he'd go on and be a special player," Rea said. Each player also received a team-autographed Toros stick for participating.

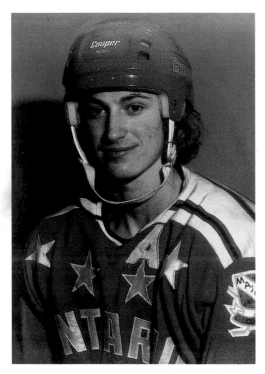

experiences of that athletic childhood. For every person in Brantford who marvelled at Wayne's talent there was another who was supremely jealous of his ability.

He was nicknamed the "White Tornado" because he wore white gloves for a year, not to be showy but because they were light and fit comfortably. His coach was his uncle (Phyllis's brother Bob Hockin) and he incurred the wrath of parents throughout the league, playing Wayne on defence and forward, double-shifting him late in close games, putting him out on the power-play or short-handed, usually running his playing time to 40 minutes in a 45-minute game. Off ice Wayne would often swap team jackets with goalie Greg Stefan — a future NHLer himself — so as to avoid attention. "I know that some say he has played too often," coach Hockin admitted, "but every time he's out there he's a threat because he controls the game." Control it he did, to such an extent that when one person kept count in a game against the Don Valley Jack's Pack, Gretzky had 18 of the team's 31 shots.

As a result of his 378-goal season, 11-year old Wayne was invited to be a guest at the Kiwanis "Great Men of Sports" Dinner in his own town. The head table included Joe Thiesman, Rudy Pilous, Angelo Mosca, and his hero Gordie Howe. Howe told Gretzky to keep working on his backhand, and after dinner when young Wayne was called to the microphone unexpectedly to say a few words, Mr. Hockey helped the White Tornado again. He got up, put his arms around the nervous boy, and declared that anyone who had done what he had already done didn't need to say a word. Wayne heaved a great little sigh of relief, and the gesture confirmed in his mind why Howe was the greatest. He learned from that banquet not only about play around the net and the importance of a backhand, but also firsthand about the value of public appearances and the qualities of sportsmanship, dedication, and manners that were required for a player to be truly great.

In the fall of 1972, Wayne moved up to Peewee for two years, playing for Turkstra Lumber and scoring 105 and then 192 goals. A year in bantam for the Charcon Chargers (where he scored 90 goals) was his last year of hockey in Brantford, though not before he got his first taste of the international arena. His team travelled to Quebec City for a tournament, and there he quickly earned accolades usually reserved in the French press for Quebeçois players. He was given the nickname Le Grand Gretzky, and he had fans chanting his name during games and lining up outside the team's dressing-room after waiting for autographs. He was 13 years old.

ONTARIO HAS DEVELOPED MORE NHL PLAYERS than any other province or country. Its various minor leagues and junior teams are the most successful in the world, and the MTHL (Metropolitan Toronto Hockey League) is the world's largest minor hockey association. With such incredible success, however, comes political intrigue and battles of ego, and like many a player, Gretzky got caught in the system at the age of 14. His parents wanted their eldest born to play in Toronto, and to that end they arranged for his billets in the city — Bill and Rita Cornish — to become his legal guardians.

He enrolled in school and transferred leagues according to the rules of the Brantford Minor Hockey Association. However, the BMHA was under the jurisdiction of the Ontario MHA, and the OMHA had not agreed to his transfer to the Young

The only extant photo of Gretzky from the 1976–77 season as a member of the Peterborough Petes. During his early years, he frequently used a stick with no tape on it at all.

Nats, of which Cornish was the manager. The OMHA decreed that Wayne play in his home city or not at all. (The OMHA also objected to the Young Nats recruiting Brian Rorabeck, a native of Brighton. That Gretzky went on to immortality and Rorabeck was never heard of again is, of course, incidental yet salient to the whole issue of player control.)

Wayne refused to return to Brantford, but the OMHA threatened to take him to court to prevent him from playing with the Young Nats. His only recourse was to join the Metro Junior B team, the Vaughan Nationals, which was in a league for players older than those under the OMHA and thus not under its control. At 14, Gretzky was now going to play *four* age groups above his own, with 20-year olds. His new team included Murray Howe (Gordie's 'other' son), Bill Gardner (who went on to play for Chicago), Stu Smith (Hartford), and Wayne Thompson (Nova Scotia Voyageurs). It was also at this time he met Paul Coffey playing ball hockey.

Gretzky made the Nats, and in his first game scored two goals — one on a superb backhand which Gordie Howe must have somehow inspired, the other into an empty net — and he knew then that he had made the right decision in joining Vaughan. By the end of the year, he was voted the league's top rookie.

The next season the team changed names to the Seneca Nats, and it was during this time, as a 15-year old, that Gretzky was called up to play major junior with Peterborough on three separate occasions. The first came November 27, 1976, and the *Examiner* hailed his arrival with the headline: "The Great Gretsky (sic) With

Petes" and a full story on his arrival. The game review two days later was both full of praise and included the correct spelling of his name:

> Wayne Gretzky, known to many as The Great Gretzky, played his first Ontario Hockey Association major junior A game Saturday night with the Peterborough Petes and not only looked like he had been there the whole season but also got the game-winning assist.
>
> Gretzky, up from the Seneca Nationals of the Metro Junior B League in Toronto, fired a good pass to Tim Trimper who scored the winning goal in the Petes' 5-4 win over the Sault Ste. Marie Greyhounds. The high-scoring 15-year old took a regular shift with Trimper and Bill Leaman and the line played extremely well, not looking the least bit out of place...
>
> "I liked playing junior A hockey a lot and the real big difference is that it is so fast. We play much shorter shifts down in Toronto and that with the speed made it tiring," said Gretzky.

His next appearance came January 8, 1977 in a 5-5 tie with the Windsor Spitfires, and this time he had two assists and again played a regular shift. His final Junior A game of the season came March 3, and although he was held pointless, he again made an impact on coach Garry Young. Back in Toronto, he helped the Nats win their championship, and at season's end he was eligible for the OHA draft.

AFTER HAVING WAYNE AWAY FROM HOME for two years, his father was determined to have him play for the OHA Brantford Alexanders or a team near home. He wrote to every team outside the immediate area telling them not to draft Wayne because he wouldn't report. Peterborough wanted to use their selection — fourth overall — to draft him, and Wayne was willing to play there. The Petes made deals with Oshawa and Kitchener not to select Wayne first or second, but they didn't bother to talk to Sault Ste. Marie about the Greyhounds' third selection, figuring the Soo was so far away they wouldn't be foolish enough to take the gamble.

They took the gamble. They offered Wayne the chance to live with the Bodnar family in the Soo, whom he knew from his Brantford minor days, and the Greyhounds promised to pay four years' tuition at any North American university if he didn't make the team or was injured. Wayne agreed to go north. His new agent, Gus Badali, insisted Wayne get the number 9 jersey, the number he wore in devotion to his hero, Gordie

Howe. Number 9 was taken, though, and coach Muzz MacPherson wasn't going to take it from fourth-year forward Brian Gualazzi and give it to a rookie, even if he were named Gretzky. So Wayne started the season with #19, a barely acceptable compromise that didn't last long, and then switched to #14, an equally uncomfortable back-of-sweater assignation.

Then MacPherson recalled the trade that had sent Phil Esposito from Boston to New York at the start of the 1975–76 season. Espo had always worn number 7 with the Bruins, but Rod Gilbert had worn that number with the Rangers. Espo arrived on Broadway and unhappily took #12, but then switched to 77, using his favourite number twice. Muzz put a double nine on Gretzky's Soo jersey, and the rest, as they say, is history.

Near the start of the year, politics reared its ugly head once again. Gretzky's playing card was revoked by the OHA because the Greyhounds had not paid the required $1500 transfer fee to Seneca, an amount Nats owner Reg Quinn demanded on principle as the amount he had spent in legal fees earlier to arrange Wayne's transfer from Brantford to Young Nats (where he was barred from playing). More importantly, Quinn also demanded that if his attempts to acquire a Junior A team were successful that Gretzky's rights would revert to Seneca. The dispute was eventually settled — Gretzky didn't miss a shift — but Quinn was never granted potential rights for him. A good thing, too. Gretzky accounted for the doubling of attendance at the Soo, and the team became the biggest draw on the road.

During a game in Ottawa, Gretzky again invoked the memory of Phil Esposito. The team was trailing 4-1 with less than half a period to play. MacPherson intended to keep Wayne on the bench to rest him for the next night's game since this seemed over. But he threw him out on a power-play, and just as Espo had done on one of his first NHL shifts, Wayne looked back and said to Muzz, "Do you want me to tie it or win it?" MacPherson said a tie would be fine, and Wayne hopped over the boards and scored three goals to give his team a point.

At Christmas, Gretzky was invited to join Team Canada at the World Junior Championships held this year in Quebec City. Quebeckers embraced his presence alone, for they were otherwise miffed that the squad was without a single French-Canadian on the roster. The team, however, was one of the most talented ever to play at the World Juniors, and included Mike Gartner, Craig Hartsburg, Bobby Smith, Rick Vaive, Rob Ramage, Wayne Babych, and Tony McKegney. The 16-year old Gretzky was invited only because he was leading the OHA in scoring, and NHL scout Torchy Schell was quick to temper praise for Gretzky: "He stick-handles and passes really well and knows what to do with the puck. But by the time he's eighteen he may decide to be a doctor or something or find other interests. Mind you, if he continues playing, he'll attract a lot of attention." The team finished a disappointing third, but Gretzky led the tournament in scoring with eight goals and 17 points in six games.

He returned to the Soo in early January, and was still leading the OHA in scoring. Although he finished the season with 70 goals and 182 points, besting the previous league record, he was second to Bobby Smith of the Ottawa 67's. While the 18-year old Smith was to go first overall in the 1978 NHL Entry Draft that summer, the 17-year old Gretzky was to begin his pro career that same October, in the World Hockey Association.

TWO

GOING PRO AT SEVENTEEN

THE ARRANGEMENT BETWEEN THE NHL and the three major junior leagues in Canada was perfect. Teenagers played four years in junior and then became eligible for the NHL Entry Draft to see which team they'd play for professionally. There had been talk about drafting players who were 18 or 19, but all parties agreed that to lower the age from 20 would serve to put many teenagers in the NHL before they were ready.

All that changed with the establishment of the World Hockey Association (WHA) in 1972. WHA owners knew that by signing teen players they could beat the NHL to the best available young talent. That's how Mark Howe, Mike Gartner, and Ken Linseman all got started in the pro game, leaving Junior at age 18 to join the pirate league. And that's exactly what Wayne Gretzky did after a year with the Greyhounds, writing himself a personal services contract as dictated by Nelson Skalbania while on a white-knuckle flight to Edmonton (appropriately, it was during his year in the Soo, where he travelled to most cities by small plane, that Gretzky developed a great fear of flying).

Gretzky was not the solution to the Indianapolis Racers' many problems. Skalbania joked that attendance went up from 2100 a game to 2200, and after eight games Skalbania bailed, auctioning Gretzky to the Winnipeg Jets and the Edmonton Oilers, whichever team would cough up $200,000 first. It turned out to be Edmonton, of course, and the death of the Racers proved to be the beginning of the Oilers and the new NHL. The final deal had Gretzky, Peter Driscoll, and Ed Mio going to Edmonton for cash, and the acquisition caught the Oilers so much by surprise that when Gretzky played his first game the next night, November 3, 1978, he had to wear #20. It was the first and last time in his pro career that he was not #99.

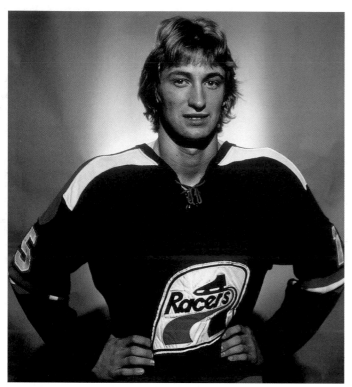

GLEN SATHER'S PLAYING CAREER was barefoot pedestrian and stoplight simple. He began his career with the Edmonton Oil Kings in Junior, played ten years in the NHL, and finished skating with the WHA Oilers in 1976–77. With 18 games left in that '76–'77 season, the Oilers fired coach Bep Guidolin and replaced him with Sather, then a left-winger with the club. Slats finished the season with a 9-7-2 record as player/coach, and the following year devoted himself full-time to bossing the Edmonton bench. In his first full year as a WHA coach, the Oilers finished in fifth place with a record of 38-39-3 and averaged just over ten thousand fans a game.

After joining the Oilers for the last 72 games of the 1978–79 season, Gretzky led the team to first place in the league with a 48-30-2 record. Attendance increased by one thousand a game, and Edmonton went to the Avco Cup finals where they lost, ironically, to the Winnipeg Jets four games to two. Gretzky led the Oilers in both goals (46) and points (110) and once again proved his ability to move up a competitive notch without missing a beat. His teammates nicknamed him Brinks (because of his lucrative contract), and as a group they represented a who's who of pro hockey, from Claire Alexander to "Cowboy" Bill Flett, and Bill Goldsworthy to Stan Weir. But the only players other than Gretzky from this WHA team who were part of the Oilers' first Stanley Cup in 1984 were two tough Daves — Hunter and Semenko.

That year, Gretzky got to play in the WHA All-Star Game, a three-game series featuring the league's Stars against the Moscow Dynamo, January 2–5, 1979. Gretzky's dream came true as he played on a line with Gordie Howe and son, Marty. Just 35 seconds into the first game, Marty — not Gordie — passed to Gretzky in front and #99 scored the first goal of the series. For the next three games, this was the greatest line in hockey.

The 35-year-old Sather was both a father and a strict taskmaster to his players. When Gretzky first got to Edmonton, he roomed with the coach until he got settled, and Slats vowed that, "One day, we're going to be in the NHL, and you're going to be

Gordie Howe and Gretzky in action during the 1979 WHA All-Star game against Moscow Dynamo. Moments after the opening faceoff, Mr. Hockey's son Mark set up the Great One for a goal.

captain of this team." Sather remembers what to him was the moment of truth in Gretzky's early development. In a game against the Cincinnati Stingers, Gretzky coughed up the puck and, in a blink, it was in the Oilers' net. Sather benched him for a period, then put him out with the team down 2-1. "He could have pouted and sulked," Sather recalled, "but when I put him back in, he scored a hat trick and we won 5-2. That, to me, was the turning point of his pro career. Not just anyone could keep his motivation."

THE KEY LEVERAGE THE WHA HAD over the NHL was the Entry Draft. The NHL held steady to 20 as the minimum age of eligibility for junior players, but in its few years of operation the WHA became notorious for pilfering the finest kids of 18 from the Canadian system. On his 18th birthday, Gretzky signed a 21-year contract with Pocklington at centre ice prior to the Edmonton-Cincinnati Stingers game, a deal intended to keep The Kid with the Oilers until 1999. Number 99 in '99: a perfect public relations pitch. After the contract was signed, the Stingers trounced Edmonton 5-2.

The WHA's signing of Gretzky itself wasn't necessarily the last straw for the NHL, but after his spectacular debut with the Oilers the NHL was worried that the best young player in the world was skating for its arch-enemy. Gretzky not only made the

WHA legitimate (as Bobby Hull had done in 1972), he scared the NHL. It was this, more than anything, that intensified merger talks that were ongoing but not yet desperate.

In the summer of 1979, an agreement was reached whereby four WHA teams could join the NHL, but all underage players (most notably Mike Gartner) were put back in the draft. Each of the four teams could protect just two players and two goaltenders, and everyone else from the WHA was available to all NHL teams in an Expansion Draft. The Oilers kept Gretzky and Bengt Gustafsson, and goalers Dave Dryden and Eddie Mio. The NHL then lowered the draft age from 20 to 19, and the following year lowered it again to 18.

While Edmonton's first year in the NHL wasn't miraculous, it certainly showed the rest of the league that, if nothing else, this was a team that could compete — and fight — with the best of them. Coach and general manager Glen Sather selected three remarkable players at the 1979 Entry Draft — Mark Messier, Kevin Lowe, and Glenn Anderson. Playing with Gretzky and Stan Weir, Blair MacDonald scored a career high of 46 goals and 94 points, second only to the Great One. And Semenko and Hunter did their parts to

ensure open ice in a safe environment for the young stable of skilled skaters.

Gretzky wasn't rountinely called the Great One just yet, though. During his first year with the Oilers, his three most common nicknames were The Franchise, The Kid, and Agent 99. But as the season progressed it became increasingly clear that he was no flash in the pan, no fake nugget or common rock. Peter Pocklington revealed that he'd been offered $2 million for Gretzky, and swore he'd reject any price for his marquee centre. "There is no price on greatness," he opined. "They'd have my head [in Edmonton] if I sold him." Time was to bear out the truth of that observation.

ON JUNE 10, 1978, GRETZKY HANDWROTE his first contract while on a plane with his father; his agent, Gus Badali; and his new boss, Nelson Skalbania. It was a four-year deal worth $575,000 and called for him to play for either Houston or Indianapolis. It also stipulated that he had to sign a formal contract on his eighteenth birthday, which he did. On January 26, 1979, prior to an Oilers-Cincinnati Stingers game, Gretzky signed a 21-year contract (retroactive to the start of the season) at centre ice of Northlands Coliseum that would make him a personal employee of Oilers' owner Peter Pocklington until 1999.

And then there were the scores. In 1978–79, before the WHA-NHL merger, there were five NHL teams that scored 300 goals. In '79–'80, there were nine, and in the next year there were 14. The Oilers scored 301 goals in their first year and 328 in the next, goals against not WHA goalies but the vaunted, supposedly superior NHL types. Gretzky, both the game's finest athlete and student, wasn't surprised by his Oilers' success, however. "Everybody in the NHL is so disciplined in their positional play," he explained, "that when you beat your man you usually got a good chance to score. In the WHA, there was a lot less positional play so you had three or four guys on your back all the time scrambling all over the ice."

Gretzky's first season in the NHL was full of highlights. He scored his first goal on Glen Hanlon at 18:51 of the third period in his third game, and that alone gave him a

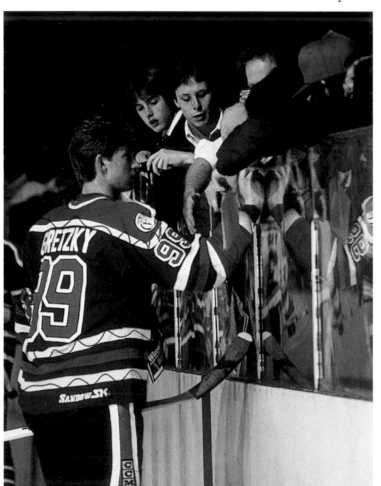

huge measure of satisfaction. "I remember thinking, 'if I never play in the NHL again, at least I scored a goal.'" At least.

He played in the All-Star Game with Gordie Howe again (though there was no fairy-tale goal), and ran neck and neck with Marcel Dionne and Guy Lafleur for the Art Ross Trophy. At 19, he became the youngest player to score 50 goals in a season. When asked about the scoring race, he humbly placed himself third in line, saying, "I don't know if I can beat Jesus [Dionne] and God [Lafleur]." But he cautiously admitted that finishing near the top of the points parade was important to him. "When we were in Toronto earlier in the year," he related, "someone wrote I wouldn't be in the top ten. When I read something like that, it gives me the drive to do what they say I can't do." To make his point, he had two goals and two assists in a 4-4 tie that night at Maple Leaf Gardens.

Agent 99 finished the season right at

the top, tied with Dionne at 137 points. Dionne got the Art Ross Trophy because years ago the NHL had instituted a rule whereby the player with the greater number of goals is named the winner in the case of a tie. Gretzky had 51, Dionne 53. Interestingly, Gretzky played 79 games, one short of the full schedule that Dionne had played. The only game he missed was on October 30, 1979, against the St. Louis Blues, when he spent a night in the hospital with tonsilitis.

While Gretzky was ever the gentleman in defeat, he did note that placing a greater importance on goals sent a bad message to youngsters. "How can you tell kids that an assist is as important as a goal? They'll have mixed emotions now. I still think an assist is as important as a goal." Life lesson: To help someone do something is as important as doing it yourself; to contribute to someone else's glory is as important as basking in your own.

Gretzky was also denied the Calder Trophy (for best rookie) because of a new rule that limited candidates to those who hadn't played in any other "professional" league. The wording was aimed directly at preventing WHA players from qualifying, but Gretzky still won the Lady Byng Trophy (for most gentlemanly play) and, more significantly, the Hart Trophy as the league's most valuable player. As the honours rolled in, Gretzky was diplomacy personified: "I suppose at the time when I was a really little kid, everyone had Gordie as his hero," he said. "I can't say I've copied any parts of his style because no one could play the game the way he does...The area where I've really tried to emulate Gordie is off the ice. He's so easy going and good with people and that's the way I hope I can be."

The Oilers qualified for the playoffs that inaugural year and faced the Philadelphia Flyers in a best-of-five preliminary round. While the result looked grim on paper — a 3-0 Philly sweep — the games told a different story. The Flyers won the series opener at 8:06 of overtime, then cruised to a 5-1 win in game two at the Spectrum. Back in Edmonton, it took two periods of overtime for the Flyers to eke out a 3-2 win and eliminate the Oilers. A sweep, yes, but hardly overwhelming.

The first season was in the books, but as the young Oilers began to develop, coach Sather could more easily see what his job was going to be: to build and define the team around the NHL's best player, a 19-year old veteran superstar named Wayne Gretzky.

THREE

YEAR TWO, AND THE RECORDS START TO FALL

THE 1980–81 SEASON OPENED LIKE EVERY OTHER for Gretzky, amid a doubting crowd and sceptical audience demanding proof that the previous season was no fluke. But while critics expected a sophomore jinx, Glen Sather was creating a team that was faster than light and younger than green. To add to his previous year's draft coups of Messier, Lowe, and Anderson, Slats drafted Paul Coffey, Jari Kurri, and Andy Moog, all of whom stepped right into the NHL that same year. With Matti Hagman and Risto Siltanen to go with Kurri, Sather also was sailing full steam ahead into European waters, not for the occasional superstar like Borje Salming or Ulf Nilsson, but as a regular source of skating-oriented, offence-minded players.

As Gretzky evolved, so did the team. Sather began the season as general manager only, hiring Bryan Watson as head coach. But the experiment lasted for only 18 games, with a 4-9-5 record, before Slats stepped in and replaced Watson. The Oilers finished the year with a disappointing record of 29-35-16. But it was a record destined to get better rather than worse, and with Gretzky on ice it was just a matter of being patient while the young players around him developed and Sather found older players to blend in and contribute. He acquired Gary Unger during the season, and Gretzky continued to take control of the game like no other player in the history of the NHL.

Just as Bobby Orr changed the game with his speed and ability to rush into play as a defenceman, so too did Gretzky's play behind the net — soon to be dubbed

"Gretzky's office" — both confound opponents and infuriate rival fans. "I started when I was in Junior B," Gretzky recalled. "I was too small — 5' 5", 110 — to stay in front of the goal, so Gene Popeil, my coach, told me to stake out some space for myself behind it, and stay off to one side."

The effect was staggering. Fans would routinely scream at their team's defence to "Get him!" but when the players tried it presented a myriad of problems. If one defenceman went to him, Gretzky came out the other side and threaded a pass to a man off the far post. If both went after him, all he had to do was flip the puck in front of the net and someone was sure to be open. If he was left there, he'd wait until one of his defencemen came in off the point. Or, he'd simply come out quickly himself — usually on his backhand — and lift the puck into the net. As a capper, just to keep everyone thinking, he'd occasionally bank the puck in off a player, as Don Cherry learned from his days coaching the Colorado Rockies. "I guess maybe I was one of the last believers," Cherry said of Gretzky's "office" skills. "We [the Rockies] were playing them the first game in Denver and Gretzky is standing behind the net. He shoots the puck in front and it goes off the defenceman. I think, 'That lucky S.O.B.' So then the next game we play them in Edmonton, darned if he doesn't do the same thing again. Altogether, he did it to us three times in four games. I became a believer."

Gretzky's other greatest asset was something for which to this day he's never been given due credit — his shot. Opposing players and coaches had trouble understanding how such a meagre body could unleash such a great shot. Bobby Hull, okay. He was a beast of a man. Orr, Esposito, Lafleur, all men of size and strength. But Gretzky? How could he generate the necessary power?

A slapshot, though, is not just about power. For starters, Gretzky had pinpoint accuracy, and was just as happy scoring along the ice as over the glove. Also, he had a huge wind-up, and while the stick hung high above his shoulders he had a knack for waiting a split second before beginning his downswing. In that moment, he made the goalie think about the possibility of a pass, and also forced the goalie to move a little more than usual, giving Gretzky more net and holes to shoot at. As fellow 50-goal man of the time Rick Kehoe said, "That shot of his is a lot harder — sneaky fast — than people think."

Gretzky's other innovation that confounded players was what Sather called his "vision," his ability to see the whole ice and to anticipate play two or three seconds

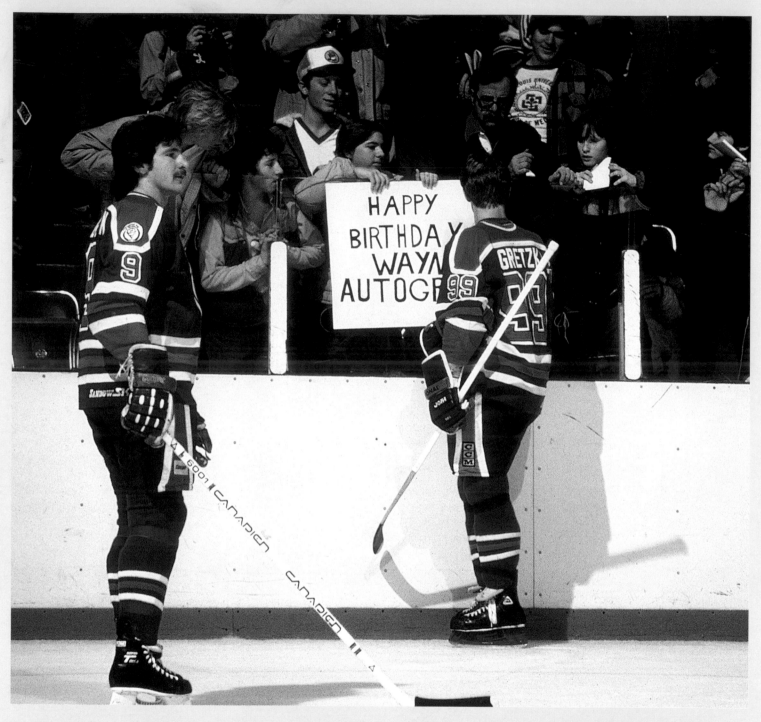

THE NHL THAT WAYNE GRETZKY LEAVES is vastly different from the one he entered, the number of teams being the least of the changes. No longer is it possible for kids to get players' autographs with such ease — the Plexiglas is too high and in most buildings children are restricted from watching the warmup from rinkside unless they have tickets there. The game has turned into a business, and the new generation of players has no devotion to a team or city, only a marketplace, and only for a fixed period of time (the length of a contract). While Gretzky's efforts have expanded the fan base in North America and the world, they have also served to make the league "big-time" in a way that makes such a simple pleasure as a railside signature a thing of the past.

before it happened. In the offensive zone, this manifested itself in a Job-like patience with the puck. He would snake in over the blueline at full speed, and as the defence-man came to him he'd curl back towards the line rather than force the play to the boards or the goal. As he turned back, he'd either feather a pass to a man going in the opposite direction — towards the goal — or he'd wait for the defenceman to back away and then move in himself. And while fans, again, screamed, "Hit him!" players

had never encountered someone who had the nerve simply to keep the puck for so long or who was so quick when someone came to him. That he could move sideways didn't hurt, either.

Long-time Boston Bruins general manager Harry Sinden elaborated: "For many years, the modus operandi in the league was to headman the puck, but Gretzky changed that. He was the first one to make the late man coming into the zone — usually Paul Coffey or Jari Kurri — the most dangerous man. Gretzky could hold on to the puck for so long, turning toward the boards and stickhandling in place, that even if you knew what he was going to do, you couldn't stop him."

What people saw from the stands and what players experienced on the ice were two different games. While it was de rigueur to go after the guy with the puck, such was no longer the case in Gretzky's NHL. Sather said that trying to hit #99 was like trying to catch confetti. Bill Torrey of the New York Islanders called him "an eel who's hard to hit because he's not around the boards much." And when Louis Sutter, father of Darryl and five other NHLers, implored his son one night to hit Gretzky, all Darryl could say was, "I'm trying! I'm trying!"

Mordecai Richler, wordsmith and hockey fan, described Wayne this way in a feature he wrote for the *New York Times Magazine* on September 29, 1985:

Both Lafleur and Orr radiated star presence, and so long as one of them was on the ice you never took your eyes off him, never mind the puck ... Gretzky is something else again. Undeniably more gifted than Lafleur, he strikes me as the first nondescript hockey star. Sometimes you don't even realize he's out there, watching as he whirls, until he emerges out of nowhere, finding open ice, and accelerating to score. Other

times, working out of a seemingly impossible angle in the corner, he can lay such a gift of a feathery pass right on the stick of whoever has skated into the slot that his teammate, startled to find the puck at his feet against all odds, will shoot wide.

It's not true that they don't run on him. The hit men seek him here, they seek him there, but like the Scarlet Pimpernel they can't board him anywhere; he's too elusive. He can fit through a key hole. Watching him out there, I've often felt he's made of Plasticine. I've seen him stretch his arm a seeming two feet more because that's what was required to retrieve a puck. Conversely, putting a shift on a defence-man, cruising very low on ice, he seems to shrink to whatever size is necessary to pass.

At the other end, Gretzky was always criticized for his defensive play. This was in part because he relied heavily on his defencemen to anticipate what was going to happen, and as soon as he saw there'd be a turnover and an Oiler would

gain possession, he would roar up ice looking for the pass. Every time someone called him a defensive liability, he'd score or set up a goal. Ultimately, having possession of the puck is absolutely the best form of defence.

GRETZKY'S 1980–81 SEASON WAS ONLY HIS SECOND in the NHL, yet it was a season for the ages, for the record book, for the doubters, for what was to become the insanity of offensive numbers registered by the highest number of them all — #99. In 1970–71, Phil Esposito, at age 29, scored an unheard of 76 goals and 76 assists, 152 points in a single 78-game season. It was a career year for Espo, though the Bruins didn't win the Cup as they had the previous year and would the next. In '80–'81, as a 20-year old,

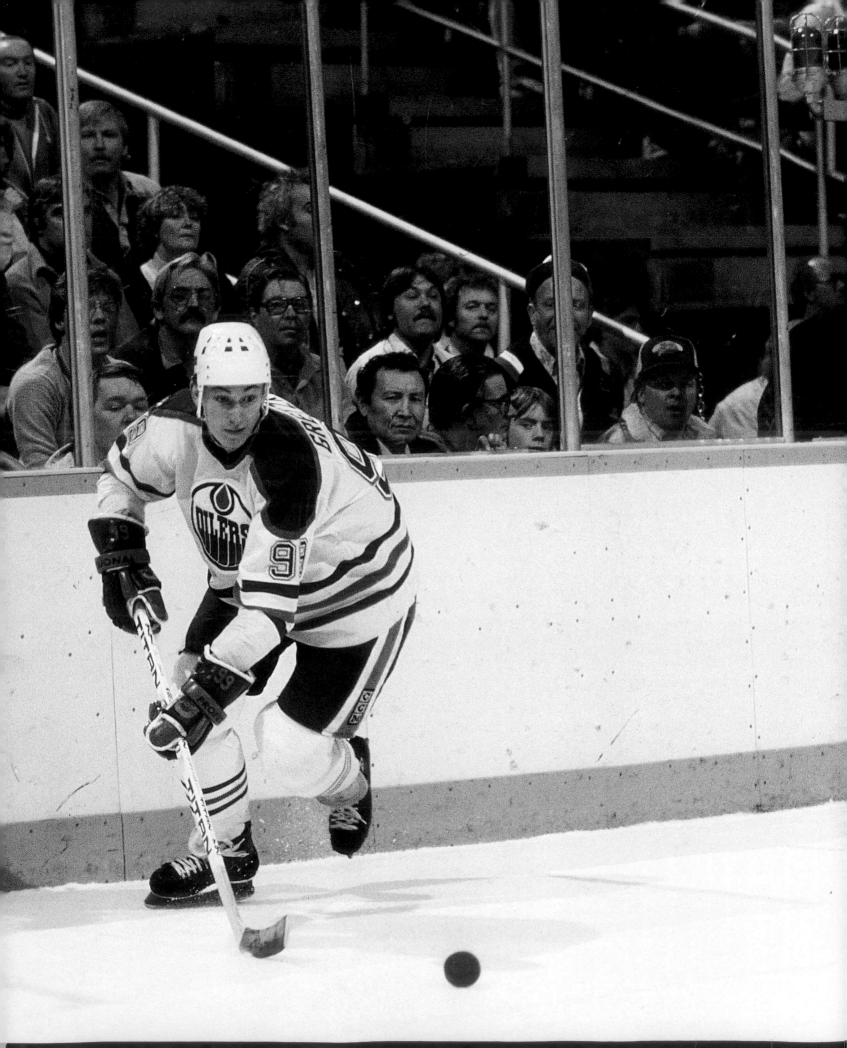

Gretzky had 164 points, breaking the all-time single-season record and, more importantly, serving notice for the future. *Everyone* talked about what Gretzky would do the following season and the season after that, as he rocketed towards his prime.

He didn't break Espo's 76-goal mark that year. Instead, his name was linked with Bobby Orr, who held the previous single-season assist record of 102. That was gone now, undone and diminished by Gretzky's 109 in '80–'81. He won his second Hart Trophy and first Art Ross (Dionne was the next closest, some 29 points back — there were no concerns about a tie that year). But as the Oilers headed into the playoffs, disaster seemed imminent. Their first-round opponent was the Montreal Canadiens,

who had finished first in the Norris Division and third overall, 29 points ahead of the Oilers with 103 to Edmonton's 14th place and 74 points.

But Gretzky read the papers. He always had. And when Habs goalie Richard Sevigny promised that his team's superstar, Guy Lafleur, would put Gretzky "in his back pocket," Gretzky's eyes lit up. In the first game of the series, on Forum ice, Gretzky tied an NHL record with five assists to lead the Oilers to a stunning 6-3 win. After the sixth goal, Gretzky skated past the Montreal bench and lightly touched the back of his pants.

In the second game, the Oilers won again, 3-1, and headed back to the Northlands Coliseum with a chance to do the improbable — sweep the mighty Habs. One overpowering 6-2 win later, they had accomplished their mission. When Gretzky was on the ice and the teams were at even strength, the Oilers outscored Montreal 11-0. Guy Lafleur, one of the dominant players of the seventies, was reduced to one innocuous assist, and clearly Lord Stanley's silver bowl was on its way from Montreal to Edmonton.

There was a stop for the Cup en route, however, and that stop was Long Island. Champs the previous spring, the Islanders now faced their eventual successors in a quarter-final series. While Edmonton had gained confidence from their free-flying Habs sweep, the Islanders knew how to win under pressure. All of their top players were in their prime, and they were not about to pave a golden path to the Stanley Cup for Gretzky and company to skate along.

The Islanders won the series in six games, and although they didn't neutralize Gretzky altogether, they did manage to hit him. Dave Langevin got him hard early on, and later Bryan Trottier took a solid run at him. But the Oilers didn't go down without a song. On the bench, they chanted, "Here we go, Oilers, here we go!" throughout the series, a gesture of self-support, confidence, and camaraderie that augured well for the future.

By the end of the series, Gretzky was worn out. In the first two games, the Isles played Edmonton hockey, wide open and offensive, and won 8-2 and 6-3. Back in Edmonton, the Oilers won 5-2 to stay in the series, but the backbreaker came the next night when Ken Morrow won the game for the Islanders, 5-4, at 5:41 of overtime. The Oilers won on Long Island 4-3, but lost the series at home 5-2. That year the New York Islanders were the better team.

Gretzky scored 21 points in nine playoff games. He was 20 years old, as were the other core members of the team. It had been a good season, but in the next year the team could look forward to the hope of a city and the promise of experience.

FOUR

THE GREAT ONE TRANSCENDS MERE GREATNESS

ESPITE HIS YOUTH, GRETZKY was profoundly aware of the importance of representing his country, of his ability to promote the game internationally and in the United States, and to create opportunities to expand hockey interest in cities otherwise not familiar with the game.

The previous year, even before the Oilers faced the Canadiens in the playoffs, Gretzky had committed himself to Team Canada and the World Championships in the event that his team lost and he could get overseas in time. As it turned out, the Oilers won and the team played too far into the playoffs to allow him to participate in the Worlds, but the 1981–82 season both began and ended with Gretzky in a red-and-white maple-leaf sweater.

When coach Scotty Bowman called him to report to Team Canada's training camp in August for the Canada Cup, Gretzky didn't hesitate, but he also knew that the cultural price would be high. "All of us on this team must realize that we're playing the next four years in the next month. If we win, then everything will be okay because the Canadian fans expect us to win. But if we lose, we're going to hear a great deal about it for the next four years, or at least until the next big tournament like this," the 20-year-old Great One said with typical maturity.

The 1981 Canada Cup was doomed before it began. The event, as organizer Alan Eagleson envisioned it, was to be held every four years, which meant the second

tournament should have been played in 1980 after the inaugural 1976 event. But when the West boycotted the 1980 Summer Olympics in Moscow for political reasons, it was impossible to plan an international hockey event to be held two months later. In fact, it wasn't until May 1981 that everything was finalized for the second Canada Cup, leaving little time for proper organization. Although Gretzky was an automatic invitee, it turned out to be the "worst experience" he ever had in hockey.

There were four coaches and four general managers on the team, and practices were gruelling: two hours in the morning, another two in the afternoon, and dry-land training to boot. The typically Canadian attitude, though, was that everything would work out just fine. In the first game of the tournament, Canada hammered Finland 9-0, and the line of Gretzky-Lafleur-Perreault was flying. It was a modest test for the Canadians, but they passed with flying colours.

Game two was more of the same, and the Edmonton-driven style of offence was now taking over the international game as well. Gretzky had two goals and two assists, and Canada outscored the Americans 8-3 (with Tony Esposito in the Star Spangled goal). Game three, though, was a hard-fought 4-4 tie with the Czechs, and the Gretzky line was held off the scoresheet. The next game, a 4-3 win over Sweden, proved disastrous when Perreault suffered a broken ankle. Earlier in the game, Gretzky had been slashed on the elbow by Lars Lindgren. "I've never been hurt that badly before in a hockey game," he said afterwards. Marcel Dionne moved to the number-one line, and in Canada's next game, a 7-3 rout of the Soviets in the final match of the round robin, the newly-formed trio accounted for eight points. An easy 4-1 win over the Americans set up the finals that everyone was hoping for — Canada and the USSR.

For half of the game, it appeared that another historic clash was in the making. The score was 1-1, and Vladislav Tretiak was playing brilliantly, keeping his team in the game time and time again as the Canadians did everything but score the go-ahead goal. Two goals near the end of the second period opened up a huge lead for CCCP, and five more in the third produced an embarrassing 8-1 result. Gretzky said of his own performance that he "played so badly they should have sent me to Siberia." This despite leading all players in scoring.

Once the tournament was over, Gretzky retreated to Florida for five days' R & R to assess his play and prepare for a new NHL season. It was during this mini-retreat that he made a conscious decision to shoot more in the coming year. He felt he had become too predictable as a passer, and as a result that he was passing up too many scoring opportunities of his own. With this plan in mind, the Oilers went on to redefine the NHL.

In goal, Grant Fuhr was heroic. As a rookie, he had a record of 28-5-14, but more importantly he instilled in his teammates a confidence to do just about anything they wanted because "Cocoa" would always bail them out. On defence, Paul Coffey was

MANY OF GRETZKY'S GREATEST GAMES and accomplishments came while wearing the red and white of his country. Although he started his international career in Quebec City as a 13-year old, his first "pro" series against the Soviets came at the 1981 Canada Cup. Although he led the tournament in scoring, Canada was embarrassed 8-1 in the finals, thanks in large measure to the outstanding goaltending of Vladislav Tretiak.

developing into the best skater the league had seen since Bobby Orr in his prime. His 89 points in '81–'82 merely scratched the surface of his rich offensive brilliance. Up front, the sky wasn't the limit so much as a decent starting point for outer space. Gretzky, Kurri, Anderson, and Messier were in a universe all their own.

Gretzky produced the most dominant season by one player in the history of the game, making even his previous record-setting season pale by comparison. He scored a ridiculous 92 goals and 120 assists, and the 212 total points was an unfathomable number for one season's worth of play. It seemed that during every game or week he was breaking an NHL record; numbers that took 65 years of NHL play to accumulate through others' hard work were being bettered with what looked like the greatest of ease by Gretzky.

On December 27, 1981, entering his 38th game of the season, Gretzky had an

On December 30, 1981 Gretzky set a record that will be one of the hardest to break. Bill Barber dives in vain to prevent Gretzky's 50th goal of the season—an empty-netter—in just his 39th game.

astounding 41 goals and 97 points. That night, against Los Angeles, he scored four times and added an assist, putting him over 100 points faster than anyone else, faster by a long shot. (To wit, his 45 goals and 102 points in 38 games would have given him the scoring title in 1997–98, an 82-game season.)

Three nights later, against Philly, he scored five times, the last time into an empty net, with Bill Barber sprawling toward the shot in an attempt to prevent history. It was his 50th goal in just his 39th game of the season. Only Maurice Richard and Mike Bossy had previously scored 50 goals in 50 games, yet Gretzky broke this remarkable record remarkably. "Wayne and empty nets," Sather remarked later. "It's like a dog in heat."

Even more astounding is to compare that scoring binge to his record the previous season. This time last year he had 17 goals and 56 points. Now he had 50 goals and 108 points. By the end of March, his torrid pace had not abated a jot. He scored 100 points in his first 38 games; he scored number 200 in his 76th game.

Coach Glen Sather could only stand behind the bench and marvel at Gretzky's accomplishments. "There is no one area that makes him superior," he said. "It's a unique combination of all areas. Technically, he is the best player I have ever seen. Watch him move the puck from side to side on his stick, watch him pass to the left, to

Gretzky beats Buffalo goalie Don Edwards the night of February 24, 1982 to break Phil Esposito's single-season record of 77 goals. He finished the year with 92.

the right. His hand-eye coordina-
tion is extraordinary, his reflexes
are uncanny. He doesn't look like
the fastest skater, but he plays
between Kurri and Anderson, who
are exceptionally fast, and they're
never ahead of him ... where he's
unmatched is in the reflexes, the
split-second acrobatics, in doing
instantly what his brain says has got
to be done."

Sather should have taken more
of the credit. It was he who played
Gretzky not only on every power-
play but also when short-handed,
giving him both the ice time and the
opportunity to rack up the points.
The Oilers were so fast and skilled in

open ice that even if they were down a man, the extra space was to their advantage.
Previously, the league had known great penalty-killers like Dave Keon and Bob
Gainey, men who would rag the puck and, as the job suggested, kill time off the clock.
Sather ignored that tactic; with the team he had, he interpreted a short-handed
situation as a time to take advantage of the extra skating room, to catch the other team
off guard, and to look for scoring chances. Of Gretzky's 92 goals that year, six came
with his team down a man.

As every hockey player will recite with precision, individual regular-season
achievements mean nothing if you don't perform under the big top — the Stanley
Cup playoffs. And while the brilliant young Oilers had performed unimaginable feats
during the regular season, the team absolutely collapsed at a pivotal moment in their
opening-round series with the Los Angeles Kings. The first game went from a 4-1 lead
for the Oilers to a 10-8 loss. This was indicative of the best (offence) and the worst (a
casual interest in defence) features of the Oilers' play during the season that earned
them a record of 48-17-15, 111 points, and an astronomical 417 goals scored.

They rebounded for a close 3-2 win in game two, thanks to Gretzky's overtime

winner, but in the pivotal third game of the best-of-five series the impossible happened. Leading the Kings 5-0 to start the third period, the Oilers fell apart and the Kings tied the game in regulation time before winning at 2:35 of overtime. Although the Oilers won the next game 3-2, the Kings stunned the Oilers in Edmonton again, 7-4, and eliminated one of the Stanley Cup favourites. A season of records and celebration had been obliterated in just five post-season games.

During the Kings' improbable third-period comeback in game three, Gretzky incurred the wrath of his detractors on two fronts. During a brawl that saw all players on the ice pair off, Gretzky alone heeded the call of referee Ron Fournier to leave the two main fighters alone. Those who didn't risked a 10-minute misconduct. And so it was that Gretzky stood at centre ice while four Oilers were outmanned and outfought by five Kings, all nine of whom received misconducts. Jay Wells of Los Angeles echoed the thoughts of the many fans watching on TV and in the L.A. crowd chanting, "Gretzky sucks!" when he commented afterwards, "He's just a player who likes to score goals, but I consider him one of the worst team men in the league."

Others on Los Angeles called him a crybaby because of his penchant for whining to officials. The fans in L.A. riled Gretzky in much the same way Calgary Flames fans used the term "pull a Wayner" for any player who fell too easily to the ice, such was their disrespect for Gretzky's ability to draw borderline penalties. For his part, Gretzky made no apologies. "I have to create room for myself," he said. "If a guy's going to be all over me, sure, I'll start diving. If it's called a couple of times, he'll back off a little. I don't do it for any reason other than that."

Gretzky acts as consultant and assistant coach for a night behind the Belleville Bulls bench, the Junior A team he bought into in 1982.

Though the Oilers' season was over, Gretzky was not done. He accepted without equivocation an invitation to play for Team Canada at the World Championships in Helsinki, Finland, extended to him just minutes after losing to the Kings. His last Oiler game against Los Angeles was on April 13, and he had an assist on Darryl Sittler's goal on April 15 as Canada hammered the home-town Finns 9-2. Gretzky had arrived in Finland four hours before game time.

"It was disappointing to lose [to the Kings]," he said briefly in Toronto en route from L.A. to Finland, "but I look at this as another chance, a new challenge. It's never difficult to play when you represent your country,

especially in light of what happened in the Canada Cup. Because we lost so bad in the final game, this will be a chance to redeem ourselves, a chance to prove we weren't as bad as we looked that evening. We're going to have a good team."

Good, yes, but not gold good. Canada won a bronze medal, but Gretzky was the hero of the tournament. He proved to be almost as popular and recognizable in Finland as in Canada, and he was as obliging as ever, signing autographs and posing for pictures with all who requested a brief audience with the "King of Hockey" as they proclaimed him.

While Gretzky was in Finland, the scene in Edmonton was frighteningly bizarre.

On the morning of April 20, 1982, a Yugoslav emigré, jobless and broke, burst into the home of Peter Pocklington and held him hostage. The man phoned police and demanded $1 million in $100 bills, but as the gunman and the Oilers owner waited in the house, armed police entered and confronted them. A member of the task force fired a shot, which grazed Pocklington's arm, and the kidnapper was arrested. Security in Finland immediately intensified for Gretzky, but though shaken he was never in any danger.

The 1981–82 season had been long, but for Gretzky there was little time to recoup. He flew to Moscow in late June to run a hockey clinic and help a Soviet crew finish a documentary on his life. The rest of the hot days were full of appearances and charity efforts, most notably a Wayne Gretzky tennis tournament in support of the Canadian National Institute for the Blind (CNIB). He also took the opportunity to buy a forty-five percent chunk of the Belleville Bulls for $180,000, an amount he could afford after signing a renegotiated contract worth $20 million over 15 years, the largest in league history.

Gretzky's monetary value on ice paled in comparison to what he was worth as a mass market celebrity endorsing products of all sorts. His agent, Gus Badali, who had approached Walter about representing his son while Wayne was with the Seneca Nats, arranged to have Gretzky's image everywhere imaginable. More importantly, although he endorsed a good number of hockey products, #99 attracted interest from companies and businesses that went far beyond the sports map. He did a famous 7-Up television ad with his brother Keith, in which they flicked a puck off the ice into the air and batted it away. He did spots for Bic pens and razors, though he didn't have to use the latter on a regular basis yet. Neilson chocolate bars, Titan sticks, Perfecta Blades, Jofa helmets, and GWG jeans all had a piece of the tasty commercial Gretzky pie. GWG promoted their product by referring to him as the Great Wayne Gretzky, selling millions of jeans and giving further credence to a nickname rooted in ability as well as character.

FIVE

SETTING A NEW STANDARD

T O START THE 1982–83 SEASON, the Oilers, for the first time since joining the NHL, didn't add any players from an uneventful summer Entry Draft. The only significant roster change was Sather's August acquisition of Ken Linseman from Hartford. Incredibly, Gretzky was beginning only his fourth season in the league but already the talk was about whether he should be considered the greatest player of all time.

Edmonton's regular season was almost as sparkling as the previous one. Gretzky had 71 goals and upped his season assist record to 125, and those 196 points were once again mathematically extraordinary. Messier, Anderson, and Kurri each had more than 100 points, and Coffey was approaching Orr territory with 96. The Oilers scored 424 goals and in 33 of their 80 games both teams combined for a total of ten goals or more. At the All-Star Game, writers voted goalie John Garrett as the MVP early in the third period. But, as if he were aware of this, Gretzky scored four goals in the final twenty minutes of the game and forced the scribes to change their votes and award him the traditional car. When he won the Art Ross Trophy at season's end, Gretzky did so in a way no one thought possible: he had more assists (125) than the second place finisher had points (Peter Stastny with 124).

Around the league, the Oilers were seen as such an aberration that there was as much criticism of them as praise. Hockey games, people argued, should not be won by

scores of 10-7 or 8-6 as was becoming commonly Edmontonian. But therein lay Gretzky's influence. Bobby Orr controlled the flow of the game, the very tempo of play. Gretzky was more direct; he controlled the scoreboard. If hockey games were based on the score, then positional play and short shifts and hard hits didn't amount to a hill of beans unless the score were favourable. Gretzky attacked the scoreboard more than he did the other team, but with all of the potent offence at his disposal, coach Glen Sather tried to spread the wealth around, reducing Gretzky's ice time in '82–'83 from about 26 minutes a game to 22.

"I make no bones about it," Sather admitted, "Wayne played far too much last year. And I was the one who could have cut back. But I felt I was caught up in a chapter of history. He was doing something that had never happened before and I didn't feel I had the right to stop it."

Of course, Slats's decision was based heavily on the too-short playoff run of the year before. The ultimate goal, after all, was not a 200-point season for one player but team success in the post-season. "We want to come a lot closer to winning the Cup than we did last spring," Sather continued. "To do that, you need three good lines, fresh people, and the right approach. We're working on all three."

The strategy worked to a tee. The Oilers finished with 106 points, first in their division, and then waltzed through the first three rounds of the playoffs, losing only one game of 12 to get to the finals. They eliminated the Winnipeg Jets in three straight games, then met provincial rivals Calgary in a five-gamer that wasn't even close, although the Flames did win one game 6-5. They were just as convincing in the next round as they broomed the Chicago Blackhawks in four straight to set up a Stanley Cup meeting with the defending-champion Islanders, who had beaten the Oilers in six games in 1981 on their way to a second successive Stanley Cup.

The Islanders needed a bit more effort than Edmonton to reach the finals. They eliminated Washington in four games in a best-of-five, and the Rangers and Bruins in six. Facing the Oilers, they were looking both forward and back. In the late seventies, before they won their first Cup in 1980, it was the Long Islanders who were an up-and-coming club that suffered agonizing playoff defeats caused by lack of experience. They took on the mighty Canadiens in 1976 and were hammered in five games. The next year, they lost to the Cup-winning Habs in six. In 1978, they lost to the Leafs in over-time of game seven of the semi-finals, and in '79 they got to the semis again before losing to the Rangers in the deciding game. Then the Cups began, and as they played Edmonton in '83 the Islanders knew all too well that the Oilers were a Cup team of the future, but they also had their own experience and success as a ballast against the energy and speed of the new kids on the ice block.

The '83 finals were the Oilers' biggest test to date, and they were demolished. Game one was a defensive nightmare

Perhaps the only photo of #99 without his name on the back, taken during an exhibition game against Calgary early in the Great One's career in Edmonton.

for Edmonton, won by New York 2-0. In game two, with the Islanders ahead, controversy erupted late in the game when slash-happy goalie Billy Smith chopped Gretzky to the ice. The Wayner fell down in agony — Smith got a five-minute major for lumberjacking — and Gretzky was never a factor again in the series. The Islanders won the final two games 5-1 and 4-2, and Gretzky, who had scored 12 goals in the first 12 games of the playoffs, didn't score once on Smith and had only three inconsequential assists. The Islanders had won their fourth Cup, but in the process the Oilers had learned many valuable lessons about the playoffs.

Edmonton had won pretty all year, skating freely, whizzing up and down the ice like pond hockey skate-meisters. Dave Semenko took on whoever got in the way, and the team was almost glib with success. But the playoffs weren't about pretty hockey; they were about sacrifice, determination, tenacity, and pain. "They took more punishment than we did," Gretzky said after walking past the Islanders dressing-room at the end of the series. "Guys were limping around with black eyes and bloody mouths. It looked more like a morgue in there than a champion's locker room. They dove into more boards, stuck their faces in front of more pucks, threw their bodies into more pileups. They sacrificed everything they had." Roommate Kevin Lowe concurred: "That's what wins championships. We learned the hard way."

Gretzky's off-ice life was becoming a carnival, the closest thing hockey had to *The Truman Show*. His every move was documented and photographed, captured, question-and-answered and press-conferenced to death; fresh images and sound bites were provided continuously and replayed all day long. Every city demanded heavily of his time when the Oilers arrived in town, and Gretzky was obliging to a fault. After the finals, he donated his gloves to a vault where they would be sealed in the West Edmonton Mall for 50 years. Rumours orbited the Oilers world suggesting that Peter Pocklington would sell Gretzky to the Rangers for $16 million to offset his troubled business ventures. Mattel made a Wayne Gretzky doll to appease the millions of young girls who were among his fans. He sang "The Devil Came Down to Georgia" on Alan Thicke's talk show and appeared as a bad guy on *The Young and the Restless*. His fame as a hockey star gave him the opportunity to become involved with many people outside hockey, and this is turn created a celebrity who, to many, played hockey only incidentally.

THE 1983–84 SEASON BEGAN ON October 4, 1983, not on the ice but in the Oilers dressing-room, when Lee Fogolin took the "C" off his sweater and presented it to

Gretzky's might well be called the most enduring fifteen minutes of fame in the sporting world. Here he poses with Andy Warhol in front of a silkscreen series the artist created in honour of The Great One.

Gretzky. "I don't think there's anyone more deserving or prouder to take it than Wayne because he does so much for us on the ice," Fogey said. Gretzky's acceptance speech was equally terse: "We have one goal and one goal only — and that's to win the Stanley Cup." That, perhaps as much as skill, was what separated the Oilers from the spoilers that year. Every man, every second, talked only about winning the Cup. That was why the game was played, and that alone was the goal by which satisfaction could be fully measured.

Such was coach Glen Sather's confidence in his club that he made virtually no changes during the summer. The team that had made it to the finals the previous spring was good enough for him again this time 'round, and the players felt extra confidence despite being given the sweep by the mighty Isles.

The season proceeded at breakneck speed for the Oilers, beginning with Gretzky's 51-game point streak that started on opening night and continued until late January 1984. It broke—obliterated—his NHL record of 30 games, and the excite-ment built with every game in which he got a point. Las Vegas, the very para-digm of numeric preoccupation, began making odds that he'd get a point in every game of the season. Although records are impossible to compare between sports, the public considered his point streak comparable to baseball Joe Dimaggio's 56-game hitting streak. Gretzky got a huge scare in his 44th game, his only point coming when he scored into an empty net at 19:58 of the third period against Chicago.

Earlier in the streak, in game 21 to be precise, the Oilers humiliated the New Jersey Devils 13-4 at the Northlands Coliseum, Gretzky getting eight points. Afterwards, he lambasted the opposition. "It's disappointing," he said of the Devils' management. "These guys better get their acts together. They had better start getting better personnel and start putting them on ice. It's ruining hockey. They are putting a Mickey Mouse operation on ice."

The criticism drew censure from

all quarters of the small New Jersey hockey world, partly because it was an insulting remark, partly because it didn't help the NHL's image, partly because the comment came from the world's most respected and dominant player, and partly because he was bang-on correct. Gretzky apologized many times over for the insensitive words, but when the Oilers played in Jersey on the following January 15 fans brought signs of all descriptions to protest or mock the insult. "I learned one rule out of all this," Gretzky said. "Not to criticize anyone in public." It was, perhaps, the only blemish on his otherwise spotless public-speaking image.

The streak ended with the 52nd game, against Los Angeles, though not without some bad luck. (Charlie Huddy was given a perfect Gretzky pass and had a wide-open net — he shot wide.) The Oilers, meanwhile, continued to win and score. The team finished the season with four 100-point men (Gretzky, Coffey, Kurri, and Messier, plus

GRETZKY HAS REPEATEDLY, UNWAVERINGLY, declared over the years that his first Stanley Cup was always his greatest thrill in hockey. Looking at this photograph, it's impossible not to see why. The Cup, which he revered as a boy every time he'd visit the Hockey Hall of Fame, is outside its glass casing here and about to be held aloft in Stanley Cup custom. As captain of the team, "W. Gretzky" is the first name to appear on the Cup engraving for the 1983–84 Edmonton Oilers.

There's no better time to have an older brother than when he has just won the Stanley Cup. Here Brent Gretzky gets a tour of the Cup celebrations on ice following the Oilers' victory.

Glenn Anderson with 99 points), and a record of 57-18-5. Only the 1970–71 Bruins of Bobby Orr had four players hit 100. Gretzky, of course, led the point parade with 205 despite missing six games with a shoulder injury immediately after the scoring streak ended (during which time the team was 1-5). These were the first games he had missed in four years and were testament to another skill of his — staying healthy.

Edmonton finished first overall again, but there was no celebration in the dressing-room after the final regular-season game. The attitude would be all business until the Cup had been won. Again they swept the Jets in the traditional first-round slaughter, 3-0, but in the second round, against the Flames again, they had a much tougher time of it, winning 7-4 in the seventh game. This was a victory born of maturity and respect for the challenge that still lay ahead. They waltzed past Minnesota in the semis, but there, standing proudly like an impenetrable wall in front of the Stanley Cup, were the still mighty Islanders.

What the Islanders were aware of during the previous year about the Oilers, they were now about to experience. Last year, the Oilers had been a team of the future. This year, the future was now. Edmonton won the opening game, on Long Island, by the ridiculous score of 1-0, their first and only 1-0 game of the year. After a 6-1 loss the next night, the Oilers regrouped in Edmonton where they played the next three games. They pounded out consecutive 7-2 wins, and then in game five were up 4-0 after two periods. Pat LaFontaine scored twice in the first minute of the third to give the Isles a boost and the Oilers a scare, but Edmonton preserved the lead and scored late into an empty net. "This is why we play the game!" Gretzky screamed as he squeezed the Cup lovingly, champagne stinging his eyes as players danced and sang to the sweet music of eternal victory.

The next day, Messier, Coffey, Lowe, and Gretzky took the Cup out on the town, walking everywhere with it so that the people of Edmonton could touch it, hold it, kiss it, and believe.

The Edmonton Oilers were Stanley Cup champions.

SIX

A CAREER IN FULL FLIGHT

IN THE SUMMER OF 1984, Gretzky withdrew from his own celebrity charity tennis tournament, the fourth annual, to recover from surgery to remove bone chips from his ankle. The decision, however, was made only as a precautionary measure to ensure that he could begin training shortly for the Canada Cup in August. That was his main focus. "Winning the Stanley Cup is what you play for, it's what we get paid for, it's what we live on," he said. "But it's a different feeling to play for your country."

Gretzky had a long memory with regard to his international experiences, and to date they had been mostly tainted by unpleasant results: a bronze at the 1978 World Juniors, a bad loss in the Canada Cup finals in 1981, and a bronze in the 1982 World Championships. Revenge and pride were on the line. "We can beat them," he said of the Soviets. "Our talent is as good [as] if not better than theirs." He backed up his beliefs as soon as the tournament began, scoring the first two goals against West Germany in a 7-2 win. Team Canada went on to win the '84 Canada Cup, though perhaps the only blemish was a 6-3 loss to the USSR in the round robin and then facing the Swedes — not those Soviets — in the best-of-three finals.

THE 1984–85 SEASON SEEMED one continuous flight of ecstasy, from the Stanley Cup to the Canada Cup and now a new season of wins and goals and give-and-goes. As

defenders of the Cup, the Oilers were expected to start a dynasty, and at age 23 Gretzky was just reaching his prime. Late in the calendar year — December 19, 1984 — Gretzky had six points against the L.A. Kings, including his one thousandth in the NHL. Accomplished in only his 424th career game, he set a standard that might never be broken. Previously, the fastest to reach one thousand had been Guy Lafleur, who had achieved the feat in a more normally superb 720 games. In only his fifth season, Gretzky was already starting to pass the greats in all-time scoring.

The problem was that the more phenomenal his achievements were, the more expected and less exceptional they became to the public. Gretzky often would get "just" three points in a game and was not chosen one of the Three Stars. He was no longer being judged as merely one player in the league; he was being judged by what he had already accomplished or was deemed capable of accomplishing in the future.

The Oilers scored 401 goals in '84–'85, finished first in their division, and overwhelmed the opposition in a way that was redefining greatness. Gretzky reached the 200-point mark for the third time, scoring 73 goals and 208 total points. Linemate Jari Kurri was right behind in goals with 71, and with Paul Coffey's 121 points the Oilers had three men top the century mark. Gretzky did the incredible again by

gaining as many assists as the second-place scorer Peter Stastny had total points (135). In 27 of their 49 wins, the Oilers scored seven goals or more. The numbers were staggering, the team was winning, the fans were screaming wildly with delight each night, and the end seemed many years out of sight.

Off ice, the Gretzky empire rose and rose like a commercial Tower of Babel. A board was nailed underneath the road sign that greets drivers on their arrival in Brantford. "Home of Wayne Gretzky" was added out of civic pride, and with that sign of faith, literally, the "White Tornado" was no longer considered a flash in the pan who still had something to prove. He would endure and endure for tomorrow and tomorrow.

In April 1985, for the first time in the magazine's history, *Playboy* featured a hockey player as its interview subject. The very inclusion of the profile was indicative and symbolic of Gretzky's penetrating fame. On preparing for a game, he provided

thorough details: "The night before a game, I'm always in bed before ten-thirty, eleven o'clock religiously. I'm up around eight-thirty in the morning, have a cup of tea and something light to eat, like a piece of toast, and read the newspaper. I'll go to the rink where we'll practise at ten-thirty and after practise, at about twelve-thirty, I eat. Then I spend the rest of the afternoon watching the soap operas. I go down to the rink at about four or five. When I get to the rink, I'll play ping-pong with a couple of the guys. Most of the guys show up about five-thirty except for about six of us. Ping-pong loosens me up, relaxes me, and takes my mind off what's going to happen."

As for getting dressed, he is equally regimented: "I get dressed the exact same way every day: left shin pad, left outer pad, then right, same order, left sock, hockey sock,

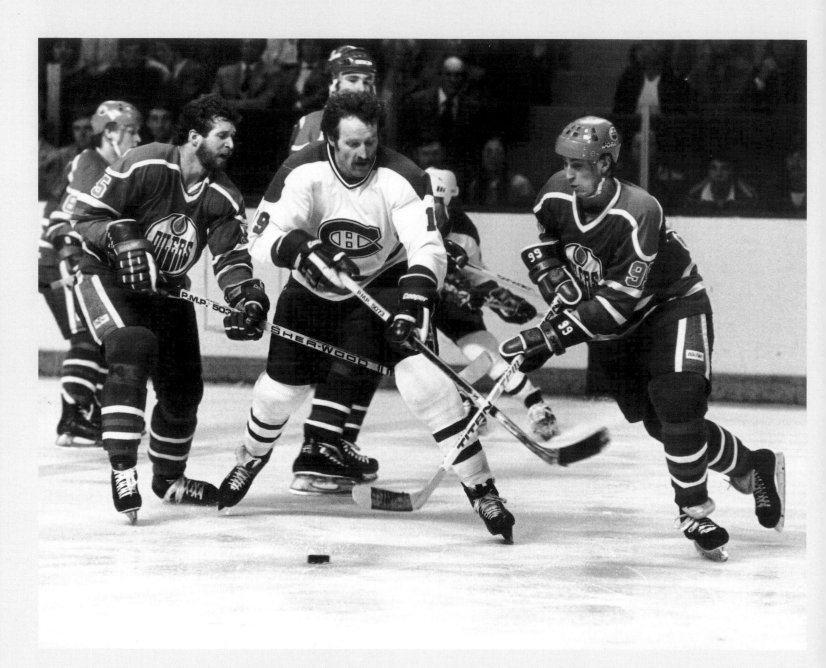

SOME OF THE GREATEST MEMORIES every hockey player carries with him for the rest of his life are of playing against other great players. Gretzky played against Larry Robinson before the end of his career, and also his idol Gordie Howe. He can boast to have played against Bobby Hull, Dave Keon, and Guy Lafleur, among other Hall of Famers. But Gretzky never played against Bobby Orr or Ken Dryden in a game. And, of course, in coming years new players who enter the league starting the 1999–2000 season will sadly say they missed playing against Gretzky.

shin pad, then pants, then left skate, right skate, shoulder pads, then left elbow pad, right elbow pad, sweater, tuck the right side in, go out on the ice for warmups, always miss the first shot wide right, come in after warmups, have a Diet Coke, an ice water, a Gatorade, then another Diet Coke."

Edmonton headed into the playoffs fully expecting to repeat as Cup champs. In the first round, they swept the Kings 3-0, but there were a couple of close calls, games one and three going into overtime. Like any great team, the Oilers got stronger as the playoffs advanced, and the next round was a 4-0 rout of the Jets. In the semi-finals,

they beat Chicago in six and outscored the Hawks 44-25. In the finals they faced the Philadelphia Flyers, the only team that had had more points in the regular season (113-109) and whom the Oilers hadn't beaten in the last eight games in Philly. Again, though, Gretzky was remarkable. All told, he had 17 goals and 47 points in 18 playoff games, and Edmonton won the Cup in five games, the last of which was an 8-3 hammering at the Northlands.

That final game didn't start out as a hammering, though. Gretzky made a sensational pass to Kurri for the opening score in the first period while being pinned to the boards by Brad Marsh. The teams then exchanged goals, but late in the period Gretzky feathered a perfect pass behind his back to defenceman Paul Coffey, who had joined the rush. Coffey beat goalie Bob Froese to make it 3-1 and then the Oilers exploded for four goals in the second to leave no doubt about the game's outcome and the Cup's destiny.

Gretzky was so accommodating to the media, to fans seeking autographs, to everyone he met in public, that even when he publicly criticized the NHL he earned respect rather than scorn. At the NHL awards dinner, where he accepted another Hart and Art Ross Trophy, Gretzky spoke out against the NHL for implementing what was called the "Edmonton Rule." Starting that October, when players received coincidental minor penalties, teams would still play five-on-five instead of one man short each. This change was made because with the extra open ice, the Oilers were scoring by the bucketful in four-on-four situations. The new rule was aimed at negating that possibility.

"I was very disappointed about it [the rule]," Gretzky said after receiving the trophies at the ceremony in Toronto. "I think the NHL is making a big mistake. I think it will bring more violence back in the game. Instead of trying to raise the level of excellence of other players, they're trying to bring the

level down. A penalty is a penalty and it should be served."

The "Edmonton Rule" didn't work out exactly the way the league had envisioned. The Oilers lost only 17 games during its first year of implementation, the '85–'86 season, scored an incredible 426 goals, and finished first overall with 119 points. And Gretzky? He had the single greatest year in the history of the game, scoring 52 goals (his lowest total since his first season) and 163 assists for 215 points. Again, he had more helpers, a lot more, than the second-place man — Mario Lemieux — had points (141). Over the 80-game schedule, he was held pointless exactly three times.

The season had greater meaning to the league as a whole. Now in his second year,

Lemieux was being hailed as the next Gretzky, the heir to Wayne's throne, the only player who could challenge Gretzky's greatness or, at the very least, put point totals on the board that came close to his. When the two met for the first time in that season, on January 22, Pittsburgh in Edmonton, the hype was sensational. Yet for all the rivalry and comparisons that were to be made in the coming years, the only real similarity lay in point totals, for Gretzky's game had little to do with Lemieux's style of play. At 6'4",

Lemieux was a greater physical presence. With his longer reach, he could challenge players one on one, not just with his quickness but with his size, and with his longer more fluid stride he was a more natural scorer. As for ability, the sophomore Lemieux had yet to earn the comparisons.

Ron Sutter put it best when he said, "You have to look at the intensity. Wayne is definitely more intense than Mario." Montreal's Guy Carbonneau provided another kind of analysis: "Mario is so big that you have to play physical against him. Against Wayne, you have to use your head a little more ... He's so unpredictable. You never know what he's up to. The only thing you can be certain [of] is that every time he's on the ice, he'll do everything he can to beat you. Mario isn't as intense." And that is the basis of a comparison that persists to this day: Mario was more naturally gifted; Wayne more dedicated and all-consuming.

DESPITE THE OILERS' CONTINUED DOMINATION of the league, their playoff run ended in shock and disappointment right in their own backyard, the Northlands Coliseum. After eliminating the Canucks in three games, Edmonton faced arch-rival Calgary in another installment in the continuing series of the "Battle of Alberta." This time, the Flames were armed and waiting, and they were helped by an enormous gaffe made by Oiler defenceman Steve Smith who celebrated his 23rd birthday by banking the puck into his own net off goalie Grant Fuhr while attempting to make a cross-ice pass in game seven. It occurred early in the third period, and made the score 3-2 for Calgary. Edmonton could not score to tie, and the dynasty was over before it had ruled for any length of time. The summer was a heavy and empty space that stood between the Oilers and the beginning of a fresh life on ice.

After such a premature end to the Cup run, a crushed Gretzky, only 25 years old, talked of retirement. "I don't see Wayne Gretzky playing for a lot longer," he said, using the third person while in the throes of post-game-seven depression. "How much longer, I don't really know. When I was 20 years old, I couldn't wait until next year. I said at the time I'd play to a certain age [30]. Now, my attitude is to take it one year at a time."

Despite the scoring records and the superb regular season, the agony of an early playoff handshake was further exacerbated by the team's only serious off-ice controversy. In the May 12, 1986 issue of *Sports Illustrated* a story condemned the Oilers for their high-society lifestyle: "One former Oiler insider told *SI* that at least five members had 'substantial' cocaine problems. Three sources told *SI* they have seen Oiler players use cocaine or marijuana at parties in Edmonton and other NHL cities." It was the most sensational scandal the hockey world had had to deal with in years, and though unsubstantiated it rocked the moral foundation of the Oilers in the public eye and the camaraderie of the players internally. The veracity of the story was never confirmed and no charges were ever laid, but it made for a doubly long and troubling summer for the Oilers.

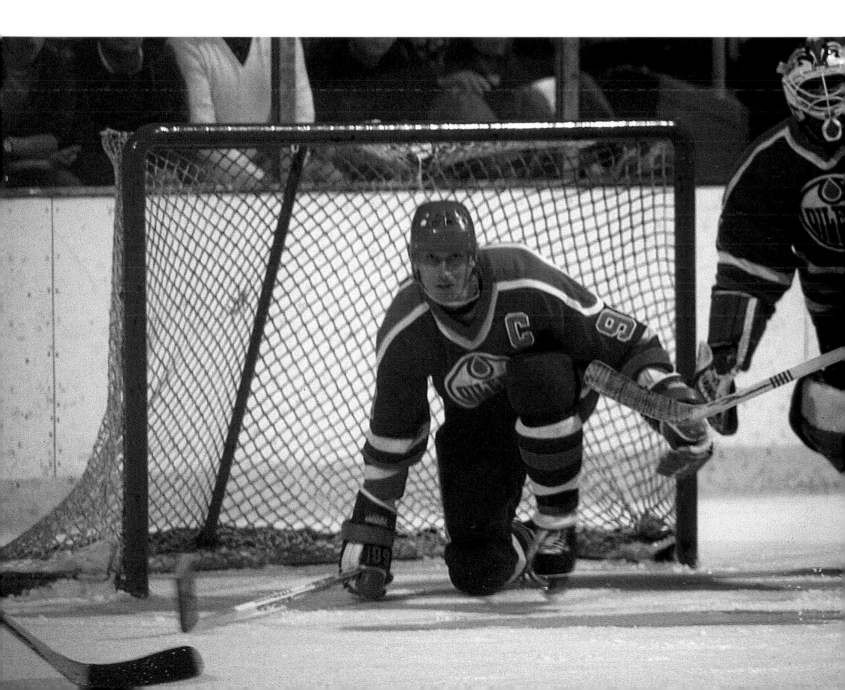

SEVEN

THE BEST AND LAST GREAT DAYS IN EDMONTON

B Y THE MID-EIGHTIES, Gretzky was heart and soul in the prime of his career. Between 1984 and 1988, he won four Stanley Cups and two Canada Cups, and scored 755 regular-season points. He was not only an established star but seemed to flourish rather than wilt after Mario Lemieux entered the league, responding again to pressure with increasingly proud performances.

Typical of coach Glen Sather's handling of the team, there were no significant moves in the off-season after the own-goal loss to Calgary in the '86 playoffs. Sather knew that having been eliminated would make them better players — and a better team — in the coming year. Although the Oilers won six fewer games in 1986–87 (50), they reached 100 points for the sixth straight year. Gretzky had 183 points, and Messier, Kurri, Anderson, Coffey, and Tikkanen all had exceptional years. The team led the league in scoring by more than 50 goals, although they had only 372, their lowest total since '80–'81.

The regular season was routinely spectacular. Edmonton paid tribute time and again to their captain as Gretzky broke record after record. Gretzky, who had done so much in so little time in the NHL, scored his 500th goal on November 22, 1986, into an empty net, in just his 575th game, far ahead of Mike Bossy's previous fastest mark of 647 games. He also scored his 1500th career point.

In February 1987 in Quebec City, the league took a breather for five days to play

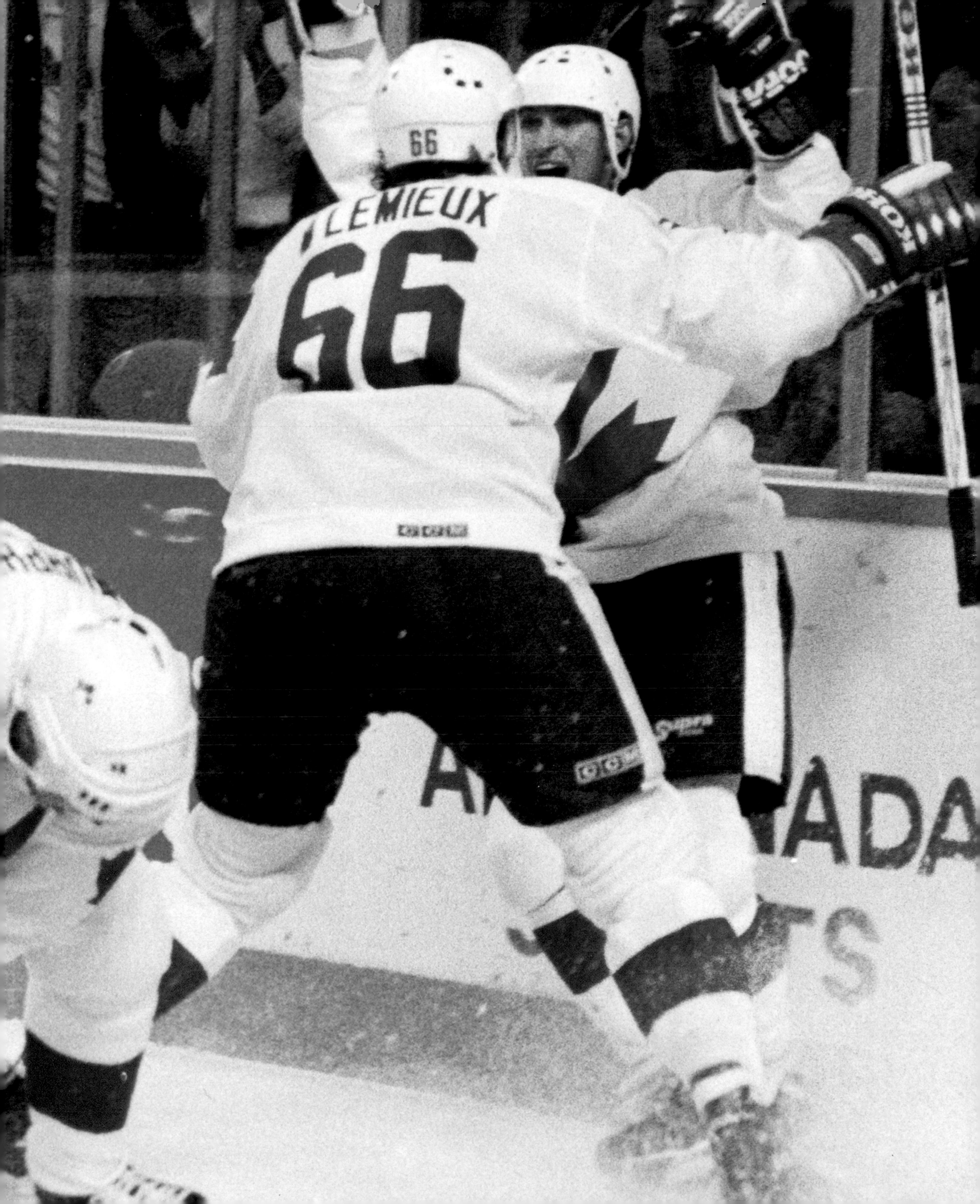

LEMIEUX
66

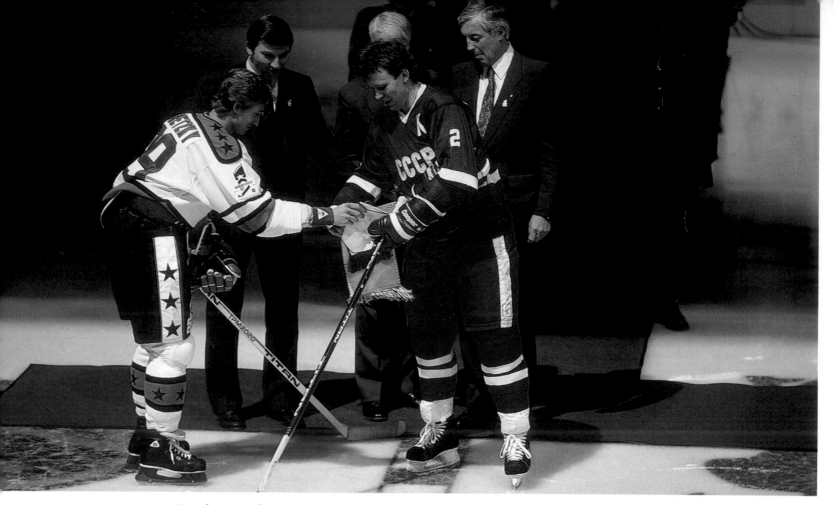

Rendez-vous '87, two games featuring the NHL's best against the Soviet Union's best. Just as the series had in 1979 in New York, these games replaced the All-Star Game, and Gretzky again dazzled in the spotlight, playing with dignity, pride, and enthusiasm. He was the best player on the ice in both games (a 4-3 win and a 5-3 loss). After a warm hug and sweater exchange at centre ice with Soviet captain and future Stanley Cup winner Viacheslav Fetisov, Gretzky called for a new eight-game Summit Series to replicate the original 1972 Series.

"Let's face it," he breathlessly enthused, "people want more than two games. And they want more than Christmas tours. And when it comes to the Canada Cup, who really wants to see Canada play West Germany? People don't want to see those other countries. People want to see Canada and Russia. I'd like to see it happen before I retire." A few months later, fans got the next best thing to a modern-day Summit Series in the form of Canada Cup '87.

HEADING INTO THE 1987 PLAYOFFS, the Oilers were more determined to win than they had been since '84. They knew that as previous Cup champions they had the talent to win, but they also knew that they were marked men, as the loss to Calgary in the previous year had proved. There would be no such mental lapses this time. They eliminated

PERHAPS GRETZKY'S FINEST hour was the 1987 Canada Cup. The best-of-three finals against the Soviets resulted in three 6-5 games, Canada losing the opener in double overtime before rebounding to win game two in double OT. In that game, Gretzky played more than 50 minutes and had five assists. But fittingly, the game's greatest passer did not score the winning goal in game three; he made a feather soft, perfectly-timed drop pass to the man he snuck a peek of over his shoulder as he crossed the Soviet blueline. Mario Lemieux skated into the pass and drilled a high wrist shot into the net for victory.

Los Angeles in five games in the first round, (now a best-of-seven series) including a 13-3 win that represented the most goals ever scored by one team in a playoff game. Winnipeg had done the Oilers a favour by beating Calgary in the first round, but the Jets' unjust reward was to be swept aside easily in four games by the Oilers in round two. The series ended on a nasty note, though, when Dale Hawerchuk slew-footed Gretzky near the end of the game. Gretzky fell heavily, hitting his lightly-helmeted head on the ice and suffering a mild concussion. But with their first semi-final game against Detroit some eight days away, he had enough time to recover. (Poor Winnipeg. They lost six consecutive series to Edmonton with a total record of 22-4.)

The Red Wings won the first game of the semis and then fell in four straight, setting up a repeat of the '85 finals featuring the Oilers and Philadelphia. Heading into the best-of-seven, Paul Coffey, who was playing his last games with the Oilers, summed up the team's performance. "In seven years, I've never seen this team play any better ... We played great when we won the two Stanley Cups, but we've got all twenty guys playing great hockey right now."

Gretzky scored the first goal in both of the first two games, each won by Edmonton, then the Flyers won game three 5-3. In game four, Gretzky assisted on three of the team's four goals in a 4-1 win. Then the Flyers rallied, winning games five and six. This set up every boy's dream, to play in game seven of the Stanley Cup finals. Just before his team hit the ice for the final game of the year, coach Glen Sather made his players' spines tingle when he said as much. "It's one thing to win a game to stay alive. But it's another to win the game that wins the Stanley Cup."

The Flyers scored the opening goal, but Mark Messier tied the game midway through the first period. It wasn't until Gretzky made another sensational pass to set up Jari Kurri in the second that the Oilers took the lead, and it turned out to be the

No fewer than nine Oilers represented the Campbell Conference at the 1986 All-Star Game (l to r: Moog, Gretzky, Anderson, Coffey, Lowe, coach Glen Sather, Messier, Fogolin, Kurri, Fuhr). Despite all their Stanley Cup glory in the '80s the Campbell-Oilers had less success at the glitter game, winning only three times in that decade.

Cup-winner. Edmonton added one goal in the third and held the Flyers to two shots in that last period, and the Cup was back in Edmonton's high-flying hands.

All through the grind that was the NHL playoffs, Gretzky took exceptional care of his body to remain in top shape. "Some of us [Oilers] have been on a special vitamin program the last three weeks," he revealed. "I don't think I've ever felt this strong." But after the Cup was won, Gretzky was so fatigued that again he talked about early retirement. "For me, personally, it was the toughest year I've ever had ... I don't know what my future holds for me right now. I'm probably more drained now than I've ever been ... One thing I want to do when I finish this game is to be able to function normally when I retire. People say there is an unwritten rule that you can't hit Gretzky, but that's not true."

SUCH COMMENTS DID NOT BODE WELL for the league. The game's premier player, in the prime of his life and in peak physical condition, fresh from the elation of having won the Stanley Cup, was talking about being so exhausted that he might retire. And, just two months later, training camp for the 1987 Canada Cup was set to open, perhaps without Gretzky. "If I cannot play my best hockey," he offered when asked about representing his country again, "then maybe I should let someone else play ... There comes a time when you have to think of yourself ... I'm going to have to sit down with Slats and my father and talk it over. Everybody has a responsibility to play in the Canada Cup, to help out the players' association, but I've played twice now. I enjoy playing, but I've got to start worrying about Wayne Gretzky or I'll be done at 28. It's time some new guys took over ... For the first time, it's not automatic."

Gretzky further intimated that his appearance at the Oilers' NHL training camp in September also was not a fait accompli. One rumour had it that he'd say no to both the Canada Cup and Edmonton, take a long vacation, and hook up with Dave King's Olympic team after Christmas. After playing in the '88 Olympics in Calgary, he'd join the Oilers for the playoff drive.

His Canada Cup participation, however, was never in doubt in the hearts of his fans. On July 15, 1987, he announced his decision to play in the tournament, but for the first time he did a little negotiating on behalf of the players. Before he committed to the team, he convinced Alan Eagleson, still the tournament's organizer, to promise there wouldn't be another Canada Cup until 1992. "I stood up for the thirty players who play in the games," Gretzky explained. "We don't want to play this every second season. It was time for somebody to take a stand that maybe we were playing these international games too often."

He also worked out an arrangement with Glen Sather. "We had only five days off after the last Canada Cup," Gretzky said of the players' quick return to their respective NHL training camps after the 1984 tournament ended. "Now we'll have at least seven to ten [days]. I think we've been guilty of forgetting our teams and our league. Without the NHL, there is no Canada Cup. I want to be able to play the best hockey I can toward the end of the season ... I want to be more rested come playoff time. My concerns were very much for myself, the Oilers, and the fans of Edmonton."

Comparisons of Gretzky and Mario Lemieux had been as much about how the players differed on and off the ice as about their similarities in style of play or success in the points standings. So when coach Glen Sather put the two on the same line in

Canada's national colours, not only were the two best players in the world skating side by side, but there was a palpable sense of excitement about how they could possibly complement each other's game. An early test of their fit came in practice one day when #99 royally chewed out #66 for not giving his all. Gretzky praised Lemieux for his talent, but criticized his work ethic in no uncertain terms. As Gretzky had done after being benched by Sather in the WHA, Lemieux drew inspiration from the tongue-lashing and developed the necessary attitude not just to do well but to be exceptional, and the positive results were manifested almost immediately.

The 1987 Canada Cup was as momentous and exciting for a new generation of fans as the Summit Series in 1972 had been for the previous one. As important? Never. But there were the two greatest players of the eighties combining to make hockey history. There was no halting start for this Team Canada as there had been in '84, and no horrific ending as there had been in 1981. This was a team of syncopated perfection from day one. The Canadians were undefeated in the round robin, and made it to the finals, as expected, to play a best-of-three aganst the dream opposition, the Soviet Union. A 6-5 double overtime loss to the Soviets in game one only heightened the drama at Copps Coliseum in Hamilton, and game two was, as Gretzky himself would later refer to it, the finest game of his life. This time Canada won 6-5, again in double overtime, thanks to a Gretzky (shot)-to-Lemieux (rebound) goal that sent the crowd into a frenzy. It was Gretzky's fifth assist of the game.

Game three was imbued with the highest drama, culminating at 18:34 of the third period when Lemieux converted a powder-soft drop pass from Gretzky to give Canada another 6-5 win. The indelible image of Lemieux hopping over the Soviet

goalie's stick and into Gretzky's slim arms, the two great giants of the game doing in this series what everyone had hoped they would do, was testament enough to the importance of those Canada Cups. Gretzky led the tournament in scoring, as he had done at every international event he'd competed in — World Juniors, World Championships, Canada Cup '81 and '84. Mario Lemieux led the tournament with eleven goals. Nine of them had been set up by #99.

PAUL COFFEY WAS gone, traded on November 24, 1987. The last image of him in an Oilers jersey was of him holding the Stanley Cup the previous spring. The next time he played in the NHL, he was with the Penguins, sent to Pittsburgh with Dave Hunter and Wayne Van Dorp by Glen Sather for Craig Simpson, Dave Hannan, Moe Mantha, and Chris Joseph. This was the first

blockbuster trade Sather had ever made, the first time he had significantly tampered with his young, and champion, Oilers. The trade was made only after Coffey refused to report to Edmonton following the Canada Cup, after owner Peter Pocklington accused Coffey of lacking courage as a player. The insult came during heated contract negotiations; Coffey felt humiliated, and refused to play for the Oilers ever again.

The loss of Edmonton's 100-point defenceman had only a small impact on a team with so much skill. The Oilers still won 44 games and had 99 points, and they still had three men near the century plateau: Kurri with 96, Messier with 111, and Gretzky his super-normal 149. Incredibly, it was also the first year that Grant Fuhr played more than 48 games in a season, despite this being his seventh sensational year in the league.

If Gretzky's point total seemed low, it was accomplished in just 64 games and put him in second place behind Mario Lemieux (168) for the Art Ross Trophy. On December 30, 1987, in a game against the Flyers, Gretzky sprained his knee as he was scoring his 573rd career goal, which moved him into an all-time tie with Mike Bossy. Diagnosed at first as a mild sprain, the injury kept Gretzky on the proverbial shelf for 13 games. "It happened as I shot the puck," he said. "Kjell Samuelsson kind of slid under me and Mark Howe blocked me. I wrenched the knee. I snapped it ... As soon as I came back to the bench, Mess asked me how I felt. I had heard it pop."

While this knee problem was serious, it did not jeopardize his participation in the All-Star Game in St. Louis, a game dominated by his point-producing adversary, Lemieux. The Magnificent One had three goals and three assists, won the MVP award, and again fuelled the debate as to whether he was already better than Gretzky or, given that he was only 22, would become better than #99.

A week after the All-Star Game, Gretzky tied Gordie Howe's all-time assist record — 1049 — in a game against the Leafs, but two nights later the injury bug, to which Gretzky had heretofore been almost immune, bit again in a frightening way. Early in an Edmonton-Pittsburgh game he was hit above the eye by an errant stick and had to be taken to hospital.

He had suffered a corneal abrasion and missed three more games, though when he returned he refused to use a visor.

Ironically, more than a year earlier he had tried wearing a shield in practice for a couple of weeks after seeing one of the most horrific cuts in a game. While on his back in front of his own goal, Maple Leafs defenceman Borje Salming had had a player's skate blade land flush on his face. He had needed almost 300 stitches to close the cut, which stretched from his forehead to his chin. "I have a whole new appreciation for face shields," Gretzky said at the time of Salming's accident. "I'll try it in practices for a few weeks. I've done it before but taken it off." Comfort before safety is always the NHL way.

Heading into the playoffs, the Oilers still ruled supreme. Gretzky was healthy again, Craig Simpson had scored 43 goals in 59 games for the Oilers since the Coffey trade, and Jeff Beukeboom was filling in nicely on the blueline, providing toughness and defensive reliability. In fact, this 1988 Edmonton team might well have been the strongest in franchise history and arguably one of the best teams of all time. Certainly their record in the post-season said as much. They beat the Jets in five games in the first round, then faced the Flames in the division final, Calgary having home-ice advantage.

Edmonton won the first game 3-1, a game Gretzky called the most important in franchise history, but the second went into overtime. Things looked grim when Mark Messier was given a penalty at 5:57, but Gretzky scored what might well have been the most important goal of his career, a short-handed overtime score at 7:54 of the first overtime to give the Oilers a 5-4 win. Back in Edmonton, the Oilers won the next two games to complete a hard-fought sweep. Of that OT goal, a blast over the shoulder of Mike Vernon from the top of the circle, Gretzky called it simply "my biggest thrill yet" in hockey. After the series, he rented a Lear jet and with Messier and Lowe flew to Las Vegas, Rodman-style, for a couple of casual days away from the rink. In the semi-finals, Edmonton won in five games over Detroit, and in the finals Boston lost its only opportunity to get back into the series because of bad luck.

The Bruins were down 3-0 in the series and playing at home in the old Boston Garden, but the game was suspended when a power failure at 16:37 of the second period prevented the game from being completed. The score was 3-3, Craig Simpson having tied the game for Edmonton only seconds before the lights went out. In a situation such as this, the rules demanded that the game be tacked on to the end of the series, so that if there were a seventh game, it would be played in Boston.

Seven games, though, was optimistic in the extreme. The teams headed back to Northlands for game four, and the Oilers claimed the Cup with a 6-3 win. Edmonton scored 21 goals in the finals, and Gretzky was in on 13 of them, including the series-winner which he scored midway through the second period of game four. To celebrate the victory after the final bell, Gretzky called all of the players and team staff to centre ice and began the tradition of having an on-ice team portrait taken with the Cup. It was an historic moment, a serendipitous gesture, a sensational impulse to share the team's celebration with the world.

And it was Gretzky's last public moment in an Edmonton jersey.

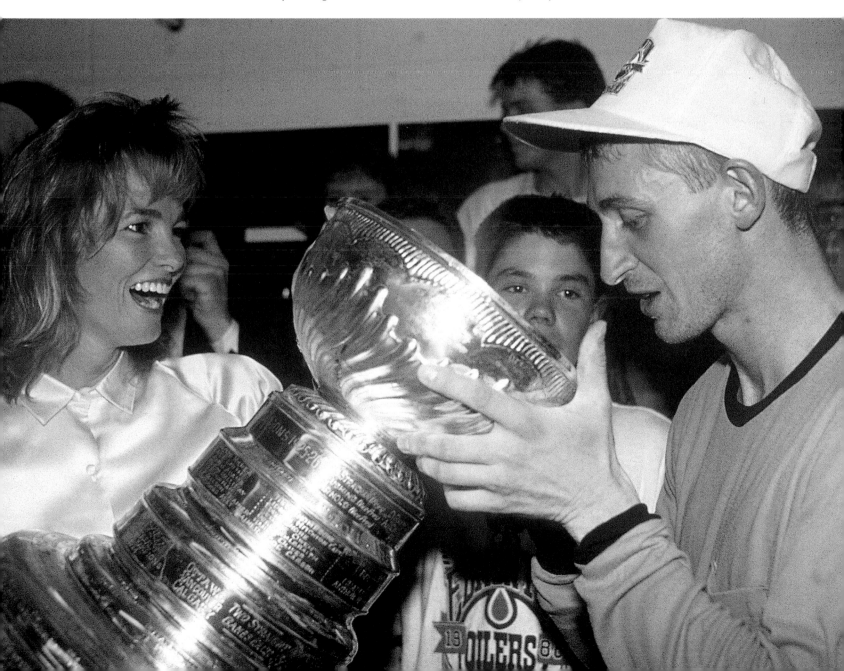

EIGHT

THE TRADE THAT TRANSFORMED THE LEAGUE

THE SUMMER OF 1988 WAS THE BEST OF TIMES and the worst of times for Gretzky, a summer of joy and misery, celebration and eulogy, passion and conflict. He had won his fourth Stanley Cup in five years with Edmonton, confirming his stature as both a great team player and the crux of a dynasty. And, he was getting married.

For almost as long as he had been in Edmonton, Gretzky had been seeing Vicky Moss, an aspiring singer and entertainer whose brother, Joey, suffered from Down's syndrome and worked in the Oilers' dressing-room. She was his first girlfriend, but they had split up more than a year before, and Gretzky's heart had since belonged to Janet Jones, a fringe Hollywood actress (*The Flamingo Kid, Police Academy 5*) and a model (semi-nude) for *Playboy*, the very magazine in which he had appeared in full interview a few years earlier.

When Gretzky had announced their engagement in February 1988, with news of a July 16 wedding date, the marriage was quickly dubbed Canada's royal wedding. On the big day, paparazzi from around the continent were out in full force. Thousands of fans lined the streets to cheer the newlyweds as they left St. Joseph's Basilica in downtown Edmonton, and the ceremony itself was a private, star-studded occasion. The couple planned to live in Edmonton, so Canadians forgave Janet being an Hollywood *habitué* via St. Louis. As Stanley Cup champion, Gretzky was truly Edmonton's mayor, model, and hero rolled into one.

The celebration did not last long, though. "It was five days after the wedding that Bruce McNall called and said that he had talked to Mr. Pocklington, that he had permission, and they had been trying to get me for two years," Gretzky said two days after being traded to Los Angeles. On August 9, 1988, Pocklington announced the deal, although it had been signed, sealed, and delivered two weeks earlier. But Peter Puck insisted that no formal press conference was to be held until after the Oilers' season ticket drive had concluded. Gretzky, Mike Krushelnyski, and Marty McSorley were L.A.-bound. In return, the Oilers received Jimmy Carson, Martin Gelinas, and first-round draft choices in 1989 (later traded), 1991 (Martin Rucinsky), and 1993 (Nick Stajduhar). And $15 million in cash.

No positive spin could be put on this story. The deal inspired controversy, charges and countercharges, public debate, and, ultimately, rage. Pocklington was pinned with the bad-guy moniker, largely because of the money he received from the Kings

FOR A NEW GENERATION OF hockey fans, primarily in the United States, hockey began not with the Original Six or even the Original 12 or 14. It began one hot day in August 1988 when Wayne Gretzky was traded to Los Angeles. With that trade, the new NHL started, one that allowed for expansion into places such as Anaheim, Phoenix, Dallas, and Florida. The new league relied on Gretzky's popularity, his undying enthusiasm for promoting the game, and his grace and skill on ice. But he leaves behind a great number of questions only time will answer in the post-Gretzky era: Has hockey established itself firmly enough in these places? Will young players help ensure the enduring success of the sport? Will those teams that relied on Gretzky for entrance into the NHL soon disappear now that he has retired?

and the public knowledge that his other business ventures needed a large injection of cash. From his new digs in Pittsburgh, Paul Coffey charged that Pocklington treated Gretzky like a "piece of meat," and many in Edmonton felt similarly disgusted and altogether betrayed.

Some blamed Janet Jones for luring Gretzky south; others said Gretzky had wanted the trade all along for selfish reasons. One thing was clear, though: The trade evoked a sense of national and cultural conflict, a sense that Canada's most famous athlete, her most beloved ambassador with no political agenda, her most gracious competitor was, like so much else economic, creative, and intellectual under the imminent Free Trade Agreement, headed south of the border.

The trade made first story not only in Canada but on every U.S. television station; the national symbolism was not lost on either sports fans or the media. Canada was losing her king. Pocklington had betrayed the country. The business of hockey was usurping its value as entertainment and athletic endeavour. In hockey terms, it was the trade of the century, yet few cared to discuss the first-round draft choices, the potential of the new, post-Gretzky Oilers, or the effect that Gelinas and Carson might have on the team. Instead, it was all about who to blame and the need to know how the owner-player relationship had deteriorated so badly that Gretzky had to be traded. Morally and ethically, Pocklington was skewered for mixing business (his failing empire) and pleasure (hockey).

Initially, Pocklington declared that the trade was entirely Gretzky's idea, prompted by his new wife and her pregnancy. "Anyone involved in a committed relationship," Pocklington began, "who wants to have a family knows that changes are brought by marriage. I truly understood when Wayne approached me and asked to be traded to the Los Angeles Kings." This despite the fact that Janet owned no property in Los Angeles, had stopped acting because of her pregnancy, and had more or less moved all of her belongings to Edmonton.

At the press conference, though, Gretzky concurred with what Pocklington said. "For the benefit of Wayne Gretzky, my new wife and our expected child in the new year, it would be for the benefit of everyone involved to let me play for the Los Angeles Kings."

Over the next couple of days, Pocklington changed his tone dramatically, saying Gretzky had an ego the size of Manhattan and that he had been faking his anguish when he had cried during the press conference. But Gretzky finally confessed that while he did ask to go to Los Angeles, he did so only after ke knew he'd be traded somewhere. "I wasn't going to let anyone tell me where I would be playing," he revealed. "I'd made that decision. I've been pleasing people all my life, so now I decided to do what's best for Wayne Gretzky. I would've liked to finish my career in Edmonton ... I offered to sign an eight-year contract. All they had to do was agree to a no-trade clause. They wouldn't do it."

Janet later elaborated on events leading up to the trade. "The day after the Stanley Cup, Pocklington told Wayne about an offer from Vancouver. Nelson Skalbania called. Wayne said to Pocklington, 'I can't believe you coming to me with this the day after we won the Cup.' Five days after the wedding, Wayne received the call from Bruce McNall. McNall told Wayne that he talked to Pocklington and Peter had told him, 'If you can swing him over, you've got him.'...That's where it all happened. Wayne saw the writing right there. You're sold. You're out of here."

AT THE OTHER END OF THE DEAL, another story was manifesting itself in Los Angeles. The Kings, after all, were the benefactors of Pocklington's money mess, the Edmonton catharsis, the trade of

Gretzky's mandate in Los Angeles expanded to encompass not only on-ice success but marketing the game throughout Los Angeles and the United States. Here #99 misses his check as a local child in Harlem skates by him and realizes a dream.

the century. Canada's loss was the Kings' gain. But talk of Gretzky heading to L.A. focused on the effect he'd have on hockey as a whole, on the city of Los Angeles, and only then on the on-ice success of the team. As soon as Gretzky went to L.A., he became a commodity, a star representative of a market. He brought the team to the front page of the newspapers, made them the talk of the town; he brought hockey talk into the social columns of L.A. papers and the glamour shows on TV.

But could he maintain such fervid interest on an ongoing basis? At first, there were sceptics, but not for long. The previous season, there had been 4500 season's ticket holders in L.A. On the night of Gretzky's first game with the Kings to start the '88–'89 season, there were 13,000. On that night, the Kings destroyed the visiting Red Wings 8-2, Gretzky getting a goal and three assists. As in Edmonton in 1979, there was no doubt that the team, the city, and the league were in the process of changing for ever.

It was as if, sans Stanley Cups, everything had been transferred from Edmonton to Los Angeles. In their first Gretzky season, the Kings won 42 games, finished fourth overall, had 23 more points than in the previous season, and were the most improved team in the league. Gretzky didn't win the Art Ross Trophy that year, but he did produce 168 points, and linemate Bernie Nicholls scored a preposterous 70 goals. Twice previously he had scored more than 40, but after he was traded midway through the '89–'90 season he never had more than 30.

Gretzky brought the stars out in Tinseltown as the likes of Goldie Hawn and Kurt Russell became regulars at the Fabulous Forum for Kings home games.

The blip in Nicholls' numbers was entirely due to Gretzky and Gretzky himself was proud, "because of what I'd contributed to my new team. I think that's what athletes need more than anything: a cause, a need to keep proving themselves over and over again." With Gretzky, Nicholls, and Luc Robitaille, who had played for Gretzky while Wayne was the owner of the Hull Olympiques before he sold the team in 1992, the Kings had a small core of highly explosive talent.

It was the most bitter of ironics that in the first round of the 1989 playoffs the Kings played the Edmonton Oilers. Motivation had always been the name of Gretzky's greatest games, and facing his old team was motivation aplenty. Just before the start of the series, he and Glen Sather got into a public argument over the trade, Sather accusing Gretzky of using it as a motivational tool for the Kings to defeat his old team, Gretzky doing nothing to prevent the emotional inflammation. "He [Sather] never thought I should have limits," Gretzky complained. "If I scored four goals, he thought I should have had five. If I got 215 points one year and only 195 the next, he said it was because I didn't care any more."

Sather shot back: "It seems to me the role of the coach is to push guys to be higher achievers, and not to be satisfied with themselves." On another occasion, he was equally passionate about his role in Gretzky's development. "It would be a crime to have the God-given talent he has and not make the most of it because you didn't push hard enough."

Gretzky also fanned the flames when he commented, "Slats has made every trade there's been [in Edmonton] for ten years. You think he didn't have a hand in this one?"

To which said Slats rejoined: "To say I traded him, or that I didn't appreciate him as a hockey player — I mean, that's ridiculous. I didn't get involved until it was three-quarters done."

In the end, Gretzky triumphed. Down three games to one to the Oilers, he almost single-handedly won the last three games to eliminate Edmonton. Gretzky had made his point. The relief and focus of winning that series was obvious, but the emotionally drained Kings were swept aside in four against the Flames in the next round.

The doubters, however, were back. They suggested Gretzky would never win another scoring championship, that the win over the Oilers was heartfelt but wouldn't be replicated, and that "Kings" and "Stanley Cup" would never be uttered in the same breath.

GRETZKY'S PLACE IN THE CONSCIOUSNESS OF HOCKEY FANS was unique. It seemed he was a legend even while he was playing, though such an accolade is usually reserved for the retired. He didn't play games so much as he broke records, and his career seemed not about about winning a face-off or anchoring the power-play so much as it was about honours and career statistics.

Yet his effect on the game was far-reaching, and his reputation filtered through every dressing-room in the league. In late August 1989, the Northlands Coliseum invited him back to Edmonton to help unveil a sculpture of himself that would become a permanent fixture outside the arena. Some fourteen thousand people attended the unveiling, including many of his former teammates in Edmonton. "When I looked at it," he commented, "I wasn't embarrassed like I thought I would be. I was elated. It represented what the team had done."

Further proof of his profound effect in expanding interest in the game came during the exhibition schedule of the 1989–90 season, his 11th in the NHL and second with the Kings. Los Angeles played three games in neutral-site rinks to spread the gospel of Gretzky, as it were. Milwaukee, Cleveland, and Denver all got to see the Great One in exhibition action, and the large crowds in each city demonstrated Gretzky's popularity and spoke volumes for his untiring efforts to popularize hockey in the United States.

Just six games into the new season, in Edmonton of all places, Gretzky set the record of all records, passing Gordie Howe as the all-time scorer in league history. Play was stopped at 19:07 of the third period after the goal against Bill Ranford, and Howe and NHL dignitaries came on the ice to honour #99 for his 1851st career point while the Northlands echoed with wild cheers reminiscent of the four Stanley Cup triumphs Gretzky had helped produce. What Gordie Howe had done in 1767 games and 26 seasons Gretzky had surpassed in 780 games and 11 NHL years. "The fact that the

One of Gretzky's investment highlights was winning a Grey Cup, in 1991, with co-owners Bruce McNall and John Candy. Here he celebrates in the Toronto Argonauts' dressing-room after the championship game at Skydome.

record was broken by someone who's such a great person takes away any sense of loss that I might have," Howe said of being relegated to number two. "I have the deepest respect for Wayne and his family and one of the best things that's happened in my life is that we're friends."

Everything about Gretzky was undergoing a glittering face-lift in Los Angeles. He and Janet frequented tony restaurants and attended glitzy parties. His friends included fellow Canadians John Candy, Alan Thicke, and Michael J. Fox, while other celebrities were now regulars at Kings games. Roy Orbison sang the national anthem at the L.A. Forum. A box seat for a hockey game took on the same California meaning as a floor pew for Magic Johnson and the Lakers. Gretzky bought horses with Bruce McNall, bought into the Toronto Argonauts football club with McNall and Candy, and was as much a social presence in the entertainment world as he was an athletic one in a Kings jersey. As an on-ice symbol of this transformation, Gretzky changed sticks, from his wood Titan to a shiny new aluminum Easton, the American stick made by human technology rather than one carefully sculpted from a Canadian tree.

"Obviously, it's a big change for me," Gretzky commented when a formal announcement was made about the stick switch. "The two things I like in a hockey stick are consistency and stiffness. I was able to get that with Titan, but I've found that the aluminum stick has that, plus it's half the weight." He didn't change the tape job, though; that would always be the same. "I use black tape that has white baby powder on it," he explained. "I find that when the puck is spinning, the black tape seems to catch it and stop it from spinning. As far as the baby powder goes, I use it because the stick will collect snow along the bottom and the baby powder stops it from sticking."

Gretzky won the Art Ross Trophy again in 1990 and 1991, but the playoffs of those years produced mixed results. In 1990, he again suffered an injury towards the end of the regular season. On March 22, he returned to the lineup after missing two games because of a groin problem and was promptly hit from behind by Alan Kerr of the Islanders. He missed the last five games of the schedule and the first two of the opening-round playoff series against the Flames. The Kings knocked off Calgary in six, but then lost three in a row to Edmonton to start the next round. Late in the first period of that third game with the Oilers, Steve Smith dealt Gretzky a clean but hard hit. Later, #99 took a Steve Duchesne shot off the left ear to the tune of 36 stitches for what he called "my first blocked shot." He returned to score a goal in the third period, but had to sit out game four with a tender back. Under the guidance of captain Mark Messier, the Oilers swept the Kings that year, and went on to win their fifth Cup of the decade.

AFTER PERESTROIKA, PLAYERS FROM RUSSIA and Czechoslovakia were more easily able to join the NHL. As a result, the international game's greatest rivalry turned from Canada–Soviet Union to Canada–United States, the mystique of the former being usurped by the geography of the latter. The 1991 Canada Cup finals reflected this change in world order, as the two North American countries faced off in the best two-of-three finals after a five-game round robin series involving six countries.

In game one, won by Canada 4-1, Gary Suter checked Gretzky into the boards from behind. Gretzky lay on the ice for several minutes, and was gone for the rest of the tournament because of a sore back. Canada won game two when, appropriately, Suter coughed up the puck at the Canadian blueline on an American power-play and Steve Larmer scored a short-handed breakaway goal to give Canada a 4-2 win in the game and a 2-0 win in the series.

(Opposite) Gretzky crashed to the ice after being checked by Gary Suter in game two of the 1987 Canada Cup finals. Moments later he was hunched over in pain and missed the rest of the series with a bad back.

As always, Gretzky led all scorers in Canada Cup '91, but his play in L.A. to start the new season was hardly Gretzky-esque. Owner Bruce McNall had scheduled an exhibition game in Las Vegas for his peripatetic Kings, and a check from the Rangers' Mark Hardy during that contest put out Gretzky's now chronic back once again. He was in the lineup on opening night, but went goalless in five games to start the 1991–92 season and said, "I'm the weak link on this team."

Hockey troubles became life troubles when Wayne's father suffered a brain aneurysm on October 16, 1991. Clinging to life, Walter was rushed to Hamilton General Hospital, and when Wayne flew home to be with his family he was greeted with words from the doctor that shook him to the bone: "He may not make it through the night." Dr. Rocco de Villiers performed life-saving surgery, but Walter's memory was for ever affected.

Gretzky returned to the Kings after missing five games, but his play didn't improve; the combination of his bad back and his seriously ill father drove his skills into the ground. "This is the end," he said mournfully. "This is the end of the end. I never, ever dreamed I could play this bad ...The whole thing just hit me. It went from bad to worse to the point where I had serious conversations with my wife about my career." But Kings assistant coach Cap Raeder told Gretzky to relax and enjoy the game, and slowly but surely Gretzky came around as his back healed and his father convalesced. The team finished the year with a decent record of 35-31-14, second in the Smythe Division, but they allowed more goals than they scored.

In the playoffs, the Oilers again beat the Kings in six games in the division semi-finals, and after Gretzky's fourth year in L.A. the doubters seemed to have won the day. He would never take the Kings very far in the playoffs.

NINE

ONE MORE TRIP TO THE FINALS

THE 1992–93 SEASON STARTED DISASTROUSLY for Gretzky and the Kings. He worked hard over the summer to stay in shape and went to training camp in good spirits. Two weeks later, he was in so much pain he had to get help. He was diagnosed with a herniated thoracic disc, a rare spinal injury that affects the ribs. Doctors thought he might miss the whole season, and even the most positive prognosis had him sitting out for at least two months before resuming physical activity. For the first time since 1978–79, the NHL would operate without the Great One, who had played, ominously, 999 career games.

At first, Gretzky's absence seemed to motivate the team, as the Kings began the year with a record of 19-7-2. Then the collapse began, and they slumped to 1-7-3 through the end of the calendar year. Gretzky returned on January 6, 1993, and from then until the season's end the team went 19-21-5 under first-year head coach Barry Melrose. As the regular schedule expired, there was little reason for optimism in Kings-land, save for the fact that Gretzky was entering the playoffs fresher than ever before. L.A. won a close first-round series against Calgary that was tied at two games each until the Kings blew the doors open, winning the last two 9-4 and 9-6 to advance to the second round.

Against the Canucks in round two, the heroics were similar but more dramatic, as they took another series tied at two games and won 4-3 (in overtime) and 5-3 to

(Opposite) Gretzky in the visitors' dressing-room at Maple Leaf Gardens after the Kings eliminated the Leafs from the 1993 playoffs and advanced to the Stanley Cup finals against the Canadiens.

eliminate the Canucks and face the Leafs, who were in the semi-finals for the first time since 1978. Gretzky, who was born just down the highway from Maple Leaf Gardens, had always loved that building more than any other in the league. Over the years, he had annihilated the Leafs on his every visit to Toronto, and in this series he was all the more motivated by the chase for the Stanley Cup. "If you can't get up for a game at Maple Leaf Gardens," he always said, "you don't deserve to play hockey."

For the first time in those playoffs, the opposition won game five in a 2-2 series, and heading back to Los Angeles it was the Leafs in control and the Kings facing elimination. In overtime of game six, Gretzky got away with a high-stick on Leafs captain Doug Gilmour, and moments later scored the OT winner to send the series to the limit. In game seven, #99 played what he later called "the best NHL game I ever played," scoring three goals and an assist in a 5-4 win and sending the Kings to the finals against the Montreal Canadiens. The Gretzky who'd be washed up at 12, out-sized at 15, and out of the NHL by 20, and who would never bring the Cup to Los

Gretzky celebrates a goal at his home-away-from-home, Maple Leaf Gardens. In this rarest of all shots, his sweater is not tucked in at the back right.

Angeles, had proved naysayers wrong. He had led the Kings to the Stanley Cup finals for the first time in franchise history.

Montreal, however, was the fresher team. Although the Kings won the first game at the Montreal Forum 4-1, the Habs went on to win three consecutive games in over-time (they won ten in a row overall in these playoffs, an NHL record) before sipping champagne from the Cup after a 4-1 win in game five in Montreal. The Kings had taken their fans on a great 24-game Stanley Cup trip, but the dream was over. (In fact, so was Gretzky's post-season in a Kings uniform.) The lustre of coach Melrose's brash tongue and Hollywood swagger, epitomized by his long hair, had worn off. The Kings finished out of the playoffs the next year. Gretzky again led the league in assists and points, but the supporting cast from the previous year was either gone or failed to pro-duce with the same consistency.

On September 25, 1993, Gretzky played the only minor league game of his career, not because he had been demoted but because he was doing promotional work for the Kings. The Phoenix Roadrunners of the International Hockey League (IHL), a minor league affiliate of Los Angeles, played an exhibition game with its NHL parent team and Gretzky was loaned to the Roadrunners for the

game along with goalie Kelly Hrudey and three other Kings regulars. The publicity was astounding, and a franchise-record 13,747 watched Wayne score two goals as the "I" team won 6-5 in an overtime shoot-out.

DURING THE NEXT NHL YEAR, one shortened to 48 games because of the owners' lockout, Gretzky pulled off a public-relations coup that no other player would have even attempted. The exhibition season began with players shaking hands after every game in a show of solidarity, demonstrating that they were united in their cause against the owners. When the season's first regular-season game was to have been played, the negotiations between NHL Players' Association (NHLPA) president Bob Goodenow and Commissioner Gary Bettman had not produced a working agreement, and portions of the season were cancelled as bargaining continued without promise, compromise, or the desire to settle. As the months passed, there was every possibility that the entire season would be lost to a "labour dispute."

Gretzky, however, produced hope where there was none, generated positive publicity where seemingly none existed, and developed ties at a time when relationships were being hacked apart. He formed the Ninety-Nine All-Stars, a group of NHLers who would tour Europe and play games against club teams on the continent for charity. The team wore old-style Detroit sweaters with the team's name on them, and showcased the league's talent abroad instead of attending meeting after irreconcilable meeting at home. The All-Stars were coached by his dad, Walter, and Doug Wilson, and were a celebration of the game and a tribute to Wayne's ambassadorial acumen. The tour was not meant to inflame the owners' ire or prove the NHLPA right; it was intended only as a way to get the players to do what they enjoyed most: play.

Throughout Europe, the reception of the Ninety-Nine All-Stars, Gretzky in particular, was mind-boggling. Even Gretzky could not have imagined how popular he and the NHL were on the other side of the Atlantic, and even the NHL couldn't have envisioned such a success during an acrimonious dispute. The All-Stars won most of their games but, more importantly, they signed autographs and ran daily clinics throughout Finland, Sweden, and Germany, and showcased the gem that was the league and its players. As a result, when the 48-game season resumed in late January 1995, the mood in hockey was optimistic rather than hostile, thanks entirely to Gretzky's efforts of diplomacy and love for the game.

In Los Angeles, however, the mood was decidedly sour. While the NHL and NHLPA were trying to hash out an agreement, Bruce McNall's financial empire — like Peter Pocklington's in Edmonton years earlier — was in the process of crashing. He filed for bankruptcy with debts in the neighbourhood of almost $200 million, and eventually pleaded guilty to trying to defraud banks, a securities firm, and the Kings of $236 million. On January 9, 1997 McNall was sentenced to five years and ten months in jail and ordered to pay $5 million in restitution damages.

The Kings played miserably after the lockout, winning only eleven games of the short season and missing the playoffs for the second year in a row. By the time the '95–'96 season was in full swing, it appeared to Gretzky that his days with the Kings might be numbered. He was entering his eighth season with L.A., but he was in the final year of his contract and would become an unrestricted free agent in the summer.

A loyal man, Gretzky felt less and less the need to commit to Los Angeles now that his friend and supporter McNall was on his way out of the Kings' office. The team was now rebuilding and it had little to offer Gretzky for the future. And, as his career seemed to be in its final stages, his desire to take one more run at the Stanley Cup increased. As the trading deadline approached, he asked to be moved.

Gretzky directs the puck into Kirk McLean's gaping net the night of March 23, 1994, scoring his 802nd career goal and surpassing Gordie Howe as the league's all-time scorer.

The Kings acquiesced, and Gretzky was sent to the St. Louis Blues, home of his good friend and right-winger Brett Hull and coached by Canada Cup alumnus Mike Keenan. In return, the Kings got Craig Johnson, Roman Vopat, Patrice Tardif, a fifth-round draft choice in 1996 (Peter Hogan) and a first-round draft choice in 1997 (Matt Zultek). Upon Gretzky's arrival in St. Louis, Shayne Corson promptly took the "C" off his jersey and gave it to #99, who thus became captain of his third team.

"I'm emotionally drained," Wayne said during his first moments in front of a

WAYNE AND JANET WITH THEIR DAUGHTER PAULINA. The Gretzkys also have two boys, Ty and Trevor, and early in the year 2000 will have another addition to the family. On June 29, 1999 they confirmed that Janet was pregnant and expecting early in the new year. At the time of the announcement, Paulina was 11, Ty 8, and Trevor 6. While the Gretzkys moved back to Los Angeles shortly after Wayne retired, he maintains significant ties with his native land, through his restaurant in Toronto, his new line of "Wayne Gretzky" clothing, and his dedication to the Canadian Hockey Association.

St. Louis camera. "I'm disappointed to be leaving Los Angeles but I'm excited to play in St. Louis. I'm thrilled to be going there. It's going to be exciting." Exciting it may have been, but the thrill was gone and Gretzky was singing the blues in no time at all. As was the case in Edmonton and L.A., he arrived to unheard-of expectations, amid flash bulbs and microphones, handshakes, questions, and smiles of celebration. His first home game with St. Louis set an attendance record at the Kiel Center, and the team's 2-0 win over Florida got the team on the right track.

In the boardroom, beginnings were equally promising. Gretzky's agent, Mike Barnett, and the Blues were close to agreeing to a three-year contract that would, in effect, ensure Gretzky finished his career with a blue note on his chest. In his second game with St. Louis, however, against the Oilers, Kelly Buchberger nailed Gretzky with an elbow that knocked him out cold and caused a mild concussion. Later in the season, Toronto's Doug Gilmour checked Gretzky to the ice. He fell awkwardly on his back and missed three games with a contusion. When Toronto and St. Louis hooked up in the playoffs a couple of weeks later, it was more of the same, the Leafs hitting Gretzky every opportunity they could.

The Blues got by Toronto, though, in six games. Gretzky again raised his play to another level at Maple Leaf Gardens, his home away from home, and St. Louis went on to face Detroit in the second round. While the series went to seven games, Gretzky's play in the first two — both losses — was suspect, as he readily admitted. "I stink," he said bluntly. "It's my responsibility to lead this team, and I consider myself responsible for both these losses." Keenan publicly agreed, especially after an 8-3 blowout in game two. "Wayne let his man go twice, and that's pretty much the end of the hockey game," he said, describing the turning point of the contest.

The Wings ultimately eliminated St. Louis in double overtime of game seven, thanks to an unbelievable bottle-popper of a slapshot by Steve Yzerman over Jon

(Opposite) The Great One stands in front of "Wayne Gretzky's", his restaurant in downtown Toronto. Located on Peter Street, Gretzky successfully lobbied City Hall to have the address of the restaurant changed to 99 Blue Jays Way.

Casey's shoulder. Keenan was critical of Gretzky throughout the series, and the combination of the public sting of those words and general manager Jack Quinn's reaction allowed Gretzky to leave St. Louis without equivocation.

"I was singled out by Mike as the guy who lost game two," Gretzky explained later. "I could handle that. That's part of his responsibility as coach, to motivate guys. But that same night, Jack Quinn, the team president, called my agent, Mike Barnett, and took the Blues contract offer off the table. The money had already been agreed to. We were just discussing the length of the deferred payments and the interest. You want to play for people who believe in you. If that's all the faith they had in me — to take a deal of the table after one bad game — right then I decided I would never sign with the Blues, which I'd had every intention of doing. Heck, I'd already put down $9000 for four season's tickets to the Cardinals."

In the end, Gretzky decided to test free agency, and ultimately joined his friend Mark Messier in New York on a team that was only two years removed from having won the Stanley Cup. This seemed to him the ideal situation, and so, on July 21, 1996, he became a Broadway Blueshirt and began the chapter that would be his last as a player in the NHL.

TEN

LAST STOP, BROADWAY

GRETZKY'S ARRIVAL IN MANHATTAN seemed a natural progression in his career. In the beginning, he had helped a new Canadian team become a dominant force in the league. Then he took on the American west coast, glitz and glamour. Because of his fame and hard work, by the time he left LA LA Land there were new NHL teams in San Jose, Anaheim, and Phoenix, and the league was entering yet another new phase of expansion. In New York, he'd be in an environment that was a combination of everything: an Original Six team, a high-profile cultural centre, a place where both hockey and celebrity were respected. New York was L.A. gone serious. It was also the place where NHL Commissioner Gary Bettman was trying to solidify the league's central office, where the ever-important marketing department was doubling and tripling in size and the league's commercial ventures were now realizing billions of dollars.

Gretzky's three years with the Rangers were awkward, full of both personal milestones and team disappointments. Particularly painful were playoff performances and international results that can't but put Gretzky's time in New York in a less than favourable light.

When he was a Ranger in name but before he played a game with his new team, Gretzky and Messier played for Canada in the World Cup, the tournament that had replaced the Canada Cup. As with the previous series in 1991, the Soviets were shut

One night, October 30, 1997, Gretzky's third jersey sported an idiosyncracy—his name was badly misspelled to read "GRETKZY."

out and the U.S. played Canada for the championship. But in the best-of-three finals the Americans prevailed in the third game in Montreal, after trailing 2-1 late in the third and then scoring four unanswered goals to claim world honours.

On Broadway, Gretzky led his team in scoring and tied for the league lead in assists in 1996–97, and in the playoffs the Rangers made an excellent run, beating Florida and New Jersey before going down to Philly in five games. In the short term, the mood at Madison Square was good. The Flyers were Cup favourites, so losing to them was no shame. In Gretzky's first year, he already had the team back in serious Cup contention, wich augured well for the next year.

But the Flyers didn't win the Cup that year — in fact, they were swept by Detroit — and in the summer Messier jumped to Canada's rainy west coast, signing a three-year deal with Vancouver after negotiations with the Rangers became volatile. Gretzky, who came to New York not only to be with Messier but to play happily as second fiddle behind his captain and friend, was now right where he didn't want to be: the dead centre of attention. At 36, he was the only marquee player on the team, but his days of 200-point seasons were over. (In fact, during one stretch of this '96–'97 season he went 21 games without a goal, the longest slump of his career.) Both Brian Leetch and Mike Richter, who had shone brightest in the World Cup, played horribly in '96–'97 and were not on the same level of celebrity as Messier and Gretzky. Although he wasn't team captain, the weight of the team was now squarely on Gretzky's shoulders.

In 1997–98, the Rangers failed to make the playoffs. During that season, the league shut down to allow all NHLers to play at the Olympic Winter Games in Nagano, Japan, and while Gretzky was Canada's best player, he was not chosen to skate in on Czech goalie Dominik Hasek during the shoot-out in the semi-finals. Canada lost 2-1, and Gretzky played his last international game a couple of days later, a bronze medal loss to Finland. "This is a crushed locker room right now and probably a crushed country," he said after the loss to the Czech Republic. "It's devastating." Just days earlier, when the Canadian team arrived at the train station in Nagano, Gretzky had been swamped by hundreds of fans. He was not just a hockey player; he was the sport personified, its grace, its beauty, its competitiveness, its sportsmanship, its skill and determination. He embodied not only all that hockey stood for, he was a pillar of Olympic excellence.

Gretzky is checked by Finn Juha Ylonen the night of February 21, 1998 in Nagano at the Olympic Winter Games.

During the sweater season of '98–'99, it became clear that the Rangers were neither a playoff contender nor a team with an immediately promising future. Gretzky alone was a beacon in the black Gotham night, but during his three years in New York one thing had become clear. He was no longer a threat based on his speed; he couldn't get open for long enough to let go his slapshot and he couldn't blow up the middle past defencemen. But his passing remained flawless, beautiful, poetic. The problem was, there were no players worthy of the puck he would put on their sticks time and again. Gretzky continued to dominate, continued to make brilliant plays, but no one

Gretzky lines up for a faceoff during the World Cup of Hockey, held in September 1996 prior to his first game as a Ranger.

could score like Coffey, Kurri, Messier, or Anderson, or even like Robitaille or Nicholls. The puck went for naught to open space or was shot wide or hopped over a stick on the deplorable, appalling ice in Madison Square Garden. Gretzky's efforts were superb but futile. In 1998–99, he missed 18 games with a team that missed the playoffs, yet still led the Rangers in scoring.

For #99, the most important day of his final season was December 19, 1998, the last time he would play at Maple Leaf Gardens. The following February, the Leafs would move out of the Gardens and into their new arena, the Air Canada Centre. Incredibly, during a 20-year career in a bloated NHL, he played only 37 regular-season and playoff games on the sacred sheet, a number his idol Gordie Howe would have accrued in any four- or five-year span. Gretzky arranged for his whole family to be at the game, and had a team picture taken after the Rangers' morning practice. "It's a horrible feeling," he said after the game, realizing he'd never skate on the Gardens' ice again, and exacerbated, no doubt, by his team's 7-3 loss.

The rest of the year didn't go much better, with the exception of a goal he scored towards the end of the season, on March 29, 1999. It gave him a record 1072 career goals in the WHA and NHL, regular season and playoffs combined, surpassing by one Gordie Howe's total. He got it with eight games to go in the schedule, and with that goal the hockey world likely was deprived of having the Great One play another season in the league.

ON SATURDAY, APRIL 10, 1999, ON *Hockey Night in Canada*, broadcaster and former goaler John Davidson suggested Gretzky might retire at season's end. It was a shocking statement, not only because of the possibility that it might happen but because the end was just a week away. And Davidson, a good friend of Gretzky's, would not have made such a statement casually. Gretzky had two big games left, Thursday the 15th in Ottawa, and Sunday the 18th in New York. By the time he arrived in Canada's capital a few days later, mayhem was the order of the day and the realization that quite likely he was about to play his last game in Canada hit hard. There was an eerie certainty to the reports, and when asked about the possibility of retirement point-blank Gretzky refused to repudiate the suggestion. Inevitability replaced scepticism, and a funereal despondency surrounded a figure who had evinced nothing but excitement, hope, and enthusiasm for twenty years.

Word spread quickly in Ottawa that this would be Gretzky's last game in his home country. The Senators brought in his entire family for the game and fans showed up at the Corel Centre plenty early to watch one last warmup and show their hero their home-made signs reading "Wayne Please Don't Retire," "Say It Ain't So, Wayne," "Just

One More Year, Wayne," and "Gretzky is God." It already had been made known that after the game Gretzky would hold a press conference.

The game itself was surreal. Gretzky had gone out of his way to save his official retirement for the city in which he currently played, but obviously the final game in Canada, the country he had represented with the utmost dignity and pride, was more important to him. Everyone at the Corel Centre was paying tribute to that which couldn't yet be acknowledged.

At game's end, the Senators' Igor Kravchuk skated to the Rangers crease to ask Gretzky for his stick. As the Rangers made their way off the ice the Senators lined up to bid adieu to Gretzky. Special handshakes that are usually reserved for playoff series-ending happiness and disappointment were this time replaced by a fond sadness all around. Gretzky would not hold the Stanley Cup again, nor would he get ready for a new training camp, a fresh September start, another season of puck-chasing. Fans stayed and cheered until Gretzky emerged from the dressing-room to acknowledge their love, and twice more he dipped in and out of the Corel Centre spotlight for sad encores. As a fitting gesture, there was no Three Stars selection that night in Ottawa, only one: Wayne Gretzky.

The Ottawa press conference was the real McCoy. Gretzky looked drained and on the verge of tears as he all but said that his career was one game from being over. "All indications are obviously pointing in that direction," he admitted. "Obviously, it's an emotional time for me; it's an experience I'll never forget tonight." In the end, he said simply that for the obvious announcement not to be made formally at a New York press conference scheduled for the next day, "it's going to take a miracle."

One miracle that almost tempted him to return was the lure of the next All-Star

During one memorable game in Madison Square Garden—October 22, 1997 versus Chicago—Janet Gretzky was knocked unconscious when a section of Plexiglas was jarred loose and landed on her. She recovered fully.

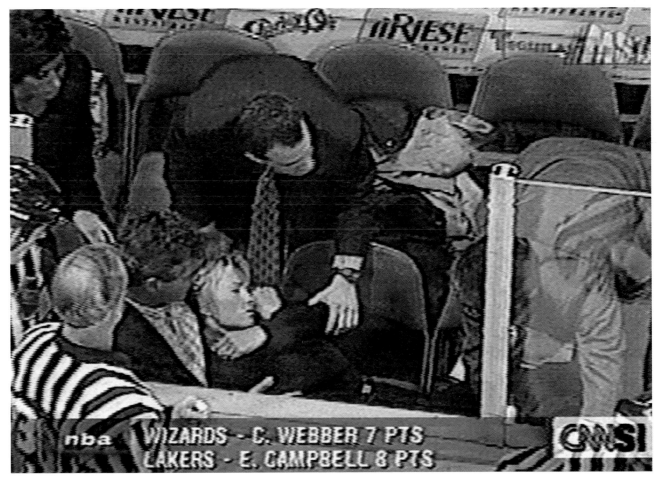

This was not how things were supposed to turn out. After one year of reunited success on Broadway with friend and teammate Gretzky, Mark Messier left the Rangers to sign as a free agent with the Canucks.

Game. "The All-Star Game happens to be in Toronto next year, and I love playing in Toronto," Gretzky reiterated. "I never had a chance to play in the new arena ... I thought about it many days. This could be a wonderful game in Toronto. I've played in All-Star games from Los Angeles to Florida, but never there." The next day he elaborated: "I'll be in Toronto for the game. Somehow, somewhere I'll be up there. But I won't be playing."

At the formal press conference at Madison Square Garden, Gretzky's opening remarks were nonetheless painful to hear articulated. "Unfortunately, sometimes you go to funerals and fortunately sometimes you get to go to weddings and fun parties, and to me this is a party, this is a celebration. I hope everyone understands that I look upon these next few days as something to really enjoy," he said, barely able to withhold tears born of two decades of NHL play. "It's obvious that today I have officially retired and Sunday will be my last game."

"In my heart, I know I made the right decision ... my gut, my heart is telling me this is the right time. A year from now, I could be in the exact same situation — everyone saying just play one more year ..." He shook his head. "I'm done. I have not wavered at all and I will never play again." Fortunately, those harsh words were followed by one last dance, against Pittsburgh on Sunday, April 18. At pre-game ceremonies, special guests filed along the red carpet to centre ice, notably Glen Sather, the man Gretzky credited for so much of his early development; Mario Lemieux, the best player Gretzky said he had played against; friend and former teammate Mark Messier; as well as his family. During the ceremony, Commissioner Gary Bettman made an historic announcement, declaring that the number 99 would be retired by the league and would never be worn by another NHLer. It was the first league-wide retired number in history and spoke volumes about Gretzky's influence and popularity, let alone his accomplishments.

The Canadian and American national anthems, sung by Bryan Adams and John Amirante, respectively, included a small tribute to Gretzky. Adams sang, "We're going to miss you, Wayne Gretzky" as the second-last line, and Amirante ended with, "O'er the land of Wayne Gretzky, and the home of the brave." Then it was time for one last opening face-off. The game itself was uneventful, save for a goal by Brian Leetch with

The Great One leaves his favourite sheet of ice for the last time, December 19, 1998. Maple Leaf Gardens would close its doors to the NHL for ever just two months later.

Gretzky getting an assist, his final NHL point. He used 51 sticks that day, signing them and giving many away to friends and teammates after the game. He wore three sweaters, one of which he kept for himself, one of which he gave to general manager Neil Smith, and the last of which he saved, most probably, for the Hockey Hall of Fame. In tribute to Gretzky's glory, the ice behind each goal — Gretzky's office — had a "99" painted on it. After the game, as had happened in Ottawa, each Penguin shook his hand, and as Gretzky took celebration laps around the rink players from both teams clapped their sticks on the ice.

In the stands, Janet cried and Walter comforted his grandchildren.

PERHAPS THE DIFFICULT PART OF ASSESSING Gretzky's career is trying to pin it down in words. Numerically, his career is easily defined and ranks first. But time and again in the hours and days following his retirement announcement, when Marty McSorley, Dave Semenko, Mark Messier, Glen Sather, Mike Keenan, or others tried to sum up Gretzky's legacy, words failed to convey meaning. It is fitting that, despite his goal-scoring record, he left the game undoubtedly as the best passer the NHL has ever seen. To that end, the most famous moment in his career might not be a goal, but his spine-tingling assist on Lemieux's Canada Cup winner on September 15, 1987.

While Gretzky redefined the use of space behind the net, other players who have followed simply are not as skilled at doing what he did. He never controlled the game like Bobby Orr, intimidated the opposition like Gordie Howe, or had the fiery inspiration of Maurice Richard. His contributions were more intangible: his love for playing; his determination to make hockey popular in the U.S., through the media, through public appearances, and through his superior play; his loyalty to his country and the league. And his vision, his ability to hang on to the puck until the perfect moment, to be calm when others panicked, to do when others planned, to finish what others could only try. Those skills can never be taught.

WHEN GRETZKY WAS AWARDED MVP honours at the 1999 All-Star Game in Tampa Bay, he became the only player since the award was introduced in 1962 to win it in his final year in the league. Of particular note in the game was his flawless pass to Mark Recchi at the side of the net for Team North America's fourth goal in the first period. It was his third MVP in All-Star competition, and he retired holding or having tied six records. Perhaps one day the NHL will name the All-Star game MVP the Gretzky Award to honour its greatest achiever.

DESPITE HIS RETIREMENT, Wayne Gretzky is still very much alive. He still loves the game and cherishes his country, and he will continue to work to make hockey succeed as the only true international sport in the world. When he gets back into the game — and it will be sooner rather than later — he will represent the NHL and the game with the same sportsmanship and dedication in a jacket and tie as he did in a hockey sweater. He will sing the game's praises and help solve its problems.

During his twenty years on ice, he was much more than just a player, and his universal popularity went far beyond his being an Oiler, King, or Ranger. In an era when hockey was too frequently called "work," he spoke of how he loved to "play." At a time

when Gary Bettman and Bob Goodenow entrenched in kids the concept of hockey as a "business," Gretzky avoided contract disputes and money problems, talking instead of the "game." In an age of athletes' egomania, he was peerlessly accessible. And in a time of merchandise and collectibles being priced rather than savoured, he gladly signed autographs for any fan who requested one. During his final press conference in New York, his words of advice only strengthened the admiration everyone had for him when he encouraged kids to play hockey for fun. "Do it because you love it," he began. "Don't do it because you want to make a lot of money at it. If you do it because you love it, and you do it because you dream of playing in the National Hockey League, then everything else will fall into place."

Gretzky is a hero, a cultural icon who is the modern-day Syl Apps, a fiercely competitive gentleman. He influenced how the average person saw hockey; he transformed the game's reputation and brought dignity to the rink by impressing fans with his skill and grace. He made the game operatic, balletic, symphonic. He made hockey cool and hip, made it more Canadian as it became more international. He was with us for twenty years, yet it was far too short a time and too quickly gone. In life, the greater the pleasure the faster time passes, and watching Gretzky play 1700 games was like watching just one second tick off a clock.

(Opposite) One last team photo, not to celebrate a Stanley Cup, but to preserve in image for ever the Great One's final NHL game.

EPILOGUE

ON APRIL 29, 1999, the selection committee of the Hockey Hall of Fame extended the obvious courtesy to Gretzky, waiving the three-year waiting period for induction. On November 22, Gretzky would join his peers and be memorialized in the building he used to visit as a kid. "I would stand there and stare at all the pictures, the sweaters and the hockey sticks," he recalled after the induction announcement was formalized. "I could never go in there enough. I never thought that one day I'd have the opportunity to be in the Hall of Fame. But dreams, I guess, come true."

In the days following his last game, the playoffs, of course, continued, and though Gretzky vowed to take a year off he was conspicuous by his presence. He dropped the puck in Edmonton the night of the Oilers' first home game of their series against Dallas and was given a deafening ovation. Days later, he attended a Boston-New Jersey game at the Meadowlands.

Then he returned to Brantford to attend the funeral of Arnold Anderson, a local radio broadcaster who had been one of the first to champion the skills of the young Gretzky. Anderson interviewed Wayne and his father for radio CKPC on January 23, 1972, when Gretzky was ten years old, and already there was an air of celebrity to the young skater. "Hockey does develop boys if they have a head on their shoulders, doesn't it?" Anderson asked Walter. "Oh, yes," he agreed. "Wayne has actually matured a lot faster than some boys his age because he's been exposed to so many different things at that early age."

Friend Brett Hull shakes hands with Gretzky after his first of what will be many official appearances, here dropping the puck in Edmonton for game three of the Stars-Oilers first-round series in the '99 playoffs.

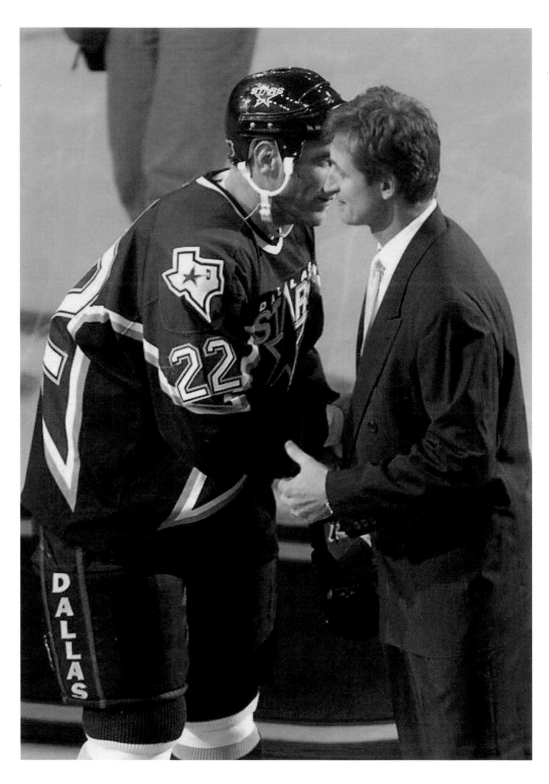

When Anderson asked Wayne if he admired any players other than Gordie Howe, he answered simply, "Gilbert Perreault." The interview concluded with the obvious question: "Wayne, would you like to play in the NHL some day if you can keep going?" To which the youngster replied simply, "Yes, I would."

Later in the playoffs, Gretzky entered Toronto's new Air Canada Centre for the first time to watch the Leafs-Penguins game, and a day later he attended Steve Chiasson's funeral in Peterborough. (Chiasson, a member of the Carolina Hurricanes, died in a single-car crash just a day after his team had been eliminated from the 1999 playoffs.) At the NHL awards in Toronto right after Dallas won the Cup, Gretzky received his last official honour — The Lady Byng Trophy. "I feel so young, maybe I can come back and play again," he joked.

Wayne and Janet were a huge hit at the Daytime Emmys in late May 1999, and later in the summer he acted as honourary spokesman for Open Ice, a summit on the state of Canadian hockey held in Toronto in August under the auspices of the Canadian Hockey Association and including the participation of Ken Dryden, Bob Nicholson, and other important hockey figures. "Nothing like Open Ice has been attempted in Canadian hockey," Gretzky explained. "It bridges the gap by bringing together hockey's amateur and professional organizations. This is more than a retrospective look at hockey or a celebration of past successes. Canadians are helping influence how our game will be played, coached, and watched in the future." On October 1, the Edmonton Oilers followed through on a long-promised honour, retiring his number prior to the Oilers-Rangers home-opener in Edmonton. Appropriately, the city of Edmonton also re-named the freeway that leads to the Northlands to Wayne Gretzky Drive.

The honours and tributes will continue for a very long time. Gretzky will be around the game the rest of his life, and ultimately he will contribute as much to hockey as an owner, executive, or NHL Commissioner as he ever did as a player.

Gretzky leaving church with Paul Coffey following the funeral service in Peterborough for the late Steve Chiasson who died in a single-car crash early the morning after the Carolina Hurricanes were eliminated from the 1999 playoffs.

APPENDIX

WAYNE GRETZKY b. Brantford, Ontario, January 26, 1961   Centre/Shoots Left — 6' 180 lbs.

		REGULAR SEASON					PLAYOFFS				
YEAR	TEAM	GP	G	A	P	Pim	GP	G	A	P	Pim
1978–79	INDY (W)	8	3	3	6	0	—	—	—	—	—
1978–79	EDM (W)	72	43	61	104	19	13	10	10	20	2
1979–80	EDM	79	51	86	137	21	3	2	1	3	0
1980–81	EDM	80	55	109	164	28	9	7	14	21	4
1981–82	EDM	80	92	120	212	26	5	5	7	12	8
1982–83	EDM	80	71	125	196	59	16	12	26	38	4
1983–84	EDM	74	87	118	205	39	19	13	22	35	12
1984–85	EDM	80	73	135	208	52	18	17	30	47	4
1985–86	EDM	80	52	163	215	46	10	8	11	19	2
1986–87	EDM	79	62	121	183	28	21	5	29	34	6
1987–88	EDM	64	40	109	149	24	19	12	31	43	16
1988–89	LA	78	54	114	168	26	11	5	17	22	0
1989–90	LA	73	40	102	142	42	7	3	7	10	0
1990–91	LA	78	41	122	163	16	12	4	11	15	2
1991–92	LA	74	31	90	121	34	6	2	5	7	2
1992–93	LA	45	16	49	65	6	24	15	25	40	4
1993–94	LA	81	38	92	130	20	did not qualify				
1994–95	LA	48	11	37	48	6	did not qualify				
1995–96	LA	62	15	66	81	32	—	—	—	—	—
	STL	18	8	13	21	2	13	2	14	16	0
1996–97	NYR	82	25	72	97	28	15	10	10	20	2
1997–98	NYR	82	23	67	90	28	did not qualify				
1998–99	NYR	70	9	53	62	14	did not qualify				
NHL TOTALS		1487	894	1963	2857	577	208	122	260	382	66

(W) = WHA

NHL TROPHIES

HART TROPHY (Most Valuable Player) — 1980, 1981, 1982, 1983, 1984, 1985, 1986, 1987, 1989

ART ROSS TROPHY (Scoring Championship) — 1981, 1982, 1983, 1984, 1985, 1986, 1987, 1990, 1991, 1994

LADY BYNG TROPHY (Most Gentlemanly Player) — 1980, 1991, 1992, 1994, 1999

CONN SMYTHE TROPHY (Playoff MVP) — 1985, 1988

LESTER B. PEARSON AWARD (MVP as selected by NHL players) — 1982, 1983, 1984, 1985, 1987

LESTER PATRICK TROPHY (contribution to hockey in the US) — 1994

MILESTONES

FIRST POINT — October 10, 1979 vs. Chicago (assist)

FIRST GOAL — October 14, 1979 vs. Vancouver (Glen Hanlon)

100th GOAL — March 7, 1981 vs. Philadelphia (empty net)

500th GOAL — November 22, 1986 vs. Vancouver (empty net)

1,000th ASSIST — November 4, 1987 vs. Rangers

802nd GOAL — March 23, 1994 vs. Vancouver (McLean)

1,050th ASSIST — March 1, 1988 vs. Los Angeles

1,851st POINT — October 15, 1989 vs. Edmonton (goal)

2,000th NHL POINT — October 26, 1990 vs. Winnipeg (assist)

2,500th NHL POINT — April 17, 1995 vs. Calgary (assist)

LAST GOAL — March 29, 1999 vs. Islanders (Flaherty)

LAST POINT — April 18, 1999 vs. Pittsburgh (assist)

MOST POINTS, ONE GAME — 8 (twice)

    November 19, 1983 vs. New Jersey

    January 4, 1984 vs. Minnesota

MOST GOALS, ONE GAME — 5 (four times)

    February 18, 1981 vs. St. Louis

    December 30, 1981 vs. Philadelphia

    December 15, 1984 vs. St. Louis

    December 6, 1987 vs. Minnesota

ALL-STAR GAME PARTICIPATION

		G	A	P	Pim
1980	Edmonton	0	0	0	0
1981	Edmonton	0	1	1	0
1982	Edmonton	1	0	1	0
1983	Edmonton*	4	0	4	0
1984	Edmonton	1	0	1	0
1985	Edmonton	1	0	1	0
1986	Edmonton	1	0	1	0
1988	Edmonton	1	0	1	0
1989	Los Angeles*	1	2	3	0
1990	Los Angeles	0	0	0	0
1991	Los Angeles	1	0	1	0
1992	Los Angeles	1	2	3	0
1993	Los Angeles	0	0	0	0
1994	Los Angeles	0	2	2	0
1996	Los Angeles	0	0	0	0
1997	Rangers	0	1	1	0
1998	Rangers	0	2	2	0
1999	Rangers*	1	2	3	0
	18 GAMES	13	12	25	0

* selected All-Star Game MVP

INTERNATIONAL CAREER

		GP	G	A	P	Pim
1978	Soviets WHA Tour	1	0	1	1	0
1978	World Juniors	6	8	9	17	2
1979	WHA All-Stars/Dynamo	3	3	2	5	0
1981	Canada Cup	7	5	7	12	2
1982	World Championships	10	6	8	14	0
1982	Soviets NHL Tour	1	2	0	2	0
1984	Canada Cup	8	5	7	12	2
1987	Rendez-vous	2	0	4	4	0
1987	Canada Cup	9	3	18	21	2
1991	Canada Cup	7	4	8	12	2
1996	World Cup	8	3	3	6	2
1998	Olympics	6	0	4	4	2

NHL RECORDS SET OR TIED

CAREER, REGULAR SEASON

GOALS — 894

894	Wayne Gretzky
801	Gordie Howe
731	Marcel Dionne
717	Phil Esposito
708	Mike Gartner

ASSISTS — 1,963

1,963	Wayne Gretzky
1,102	Paul Coffey
1,083	Ray Bourque
1,049	Gordie Howe
1,040	Marcel Dionne

POINTS — 2,857

2,857	Wayne Gretzky
1,850	Gordie Howe
1,771	Marcel Dionne
1,660	Mark Messier
1,590	Phil Esposito

Goals by a Centre — 894

Assists by a Centre — 1,963

Points by a Centre — 2,857

Assists-per-game average (300+) — 1.32

Three-or-more goal games — 50

Overtime assists — 15

Goals, including playoffs — 1,016

Assists, including playoffs — 2,223

Points, including playoffs — 3,239

40+-goal seasons — 12

50+-goal seasons — 9

60+-goal seasons — 5

100+-point seasons — 15

Consecutive 40+-goal seasons — 12

Consecutive 60+-goal seasons — 4

Consecutive 100+-point seasons — 13

CAREER, PLAYOFFS

GOALS — 122

122	Wayne Gretzky
109	Mark Messier
106	Jari Kurri
93	Glenn Anderson
85	Mike Bossy

ASSISTS — 260

260	Wayne Gretzky
186	Mark Messier
137	Paul Coffey
127	Jari Kurri
121	Glenn Anderson

POINTS — 382

382	Wayne Gretzky
295	Mark Messier
233	Jari Kurri
214	Glenn Anderson
196	Paul Coffey

Game-winning goals — 24

Three-or-more goal games — 10

SINGLE SEASON

GOALS — 92
92   Wayne Gretzky (1981–82)
87   Wayne Gretzky (1983–84)
86   Brett Hull (1990–91)
85   Mario Lemieux (1988–89)
76   Phil Esposito (1970–71)
      Alexander Mogilny (1992–93)
      Teemu Selanne (1992–93)

ASSISTS — 163
163   Wayne Gretzky (1985–86)
135   Wayne Gretzky (1984–85)
125   Wayne Gretzky (1982–83)
122   Wayne Gretzky (1990–91)
120   Wayne Gretzky (1981–82)

POINTS — 215
215   Wayne Gretzky (1985–86)
212   Wayne Gretzky (1981–82)
208   Wayne Gretzky (1984–85)
205   Wayne Gretzky (1983–84)
199   Mario Lemieux (1988–89)

Goals by a centre — 92

Assists by a centre — 163

Points by a centre — 215

Three-or-more goal games — 10 in 1981–82 & 1983–84

Goals-per-game average — 1.18 in 1983–84

Assists-per-game average — 2.04 in 1985–86

Points-per-game average — 2.77 in 1983–84

Goals, including playoffs — 100 in 1983–84

Assists, including playoffs — 174 in 1985–86

Points, including playoffs — 255 in 1984–85

Most goals, first 50 games of a season — 61 in 1981–82 &
1983–84

Consecutive point-scoring streak — 51 games in 1983–84

Consecutive point-scoring streak from start of season — 51

Consecutive assist-scoring streak — 23 games in 1990–91

Fastest to 50 goals from start of season — 39 games in 1981–82

SINGLE GAME

Assists (tied) — 7 (three times)

February 15, 1980 vs. Washington
December 11, 1985 vs. Chicago
February 14, 1986 vs. Quebec

Assists, road game (tied) — 7 vs. Washington
Assists, first-year player — 7 vs. Washington
Goals, one period (tied) — 4 vs. St. Louis, February 18, 1981

PLAYOFFS, ONE YEAR

Points — 47 in 1985
Assists — 31 in 1988

PLAYOFFS, ONE SERIES

Points, finals — 13 in 1988 vs. Boston
Assists, finals — 10 in 1988 vs. Boston
Assists, other than finals (tied) — 14 in 1985 vs. Chicago

PLAYOFFS, ONE GAME

Short-handed goals (tied) — 2 vs. Winnipeg, April 6, 1983
Assists — 6 vs. Los Angeles, April 9, 1987

PLAYOFFS, ONE PERIOD

Assists (tied) — 3 (five times)
    1st period, April 8, 1981 vs. Montreal
    3rd period, April 24, 1983 vs. Chicago
    2nd period, April 25, 1985 vs. Winnipeg
    1st period, April 9, 1987 vs. Los Angeles
    3rd period, April 12, 1987 vs. Los Angeles
Points (tied) — 4 (one goal, 3 assists) vs. Los Angeles,
    3rd period, April 12, 1987

ALL-STAR GAME

GOALS, CAREER — 13
13   Wayne Gretzky
11   Mario Lemieux
10   Gordie Howe
8   Frank Mahovlich
7   Maurice Richard

ASSISTS, CAREER (tied) — 12
12   Wayne Gretzky
      Adam Oates
      Mark Messier
      Joe Sakic
      Ray Bourque

POINTS, CAREER — 25
25   Wayne Gretzky
20   Mario Lemieux
19   Gordie Howe
17   Mark Messier
16   Ray Bourque

Goals, one game (tied) — 4 in 1983

Goals, one period — 4 in 1983, 3rd period

Points, one period (tied) — 4 in 1983, 3rd period

GAME-BY-GAME, YEAR-BY-YEAR STATISTICS
(home game for the team listed in caps)

REGULAR SEASON

1979–80 EDMONTON

DATE		TEAM	G	A	P	Pim
Oct	10	CHI	0	1	1	2
	13	Det	0	1	1	0
	14	Van	1	1	2	0
	19	Que	0	3	3	0
	21	Min	1	1	2	0
	23	NYI	0	1	1	0
	24	NYR	0	0	0	0
	26	Atl	0	0	0	0
	28	Was	0	0	0	0
	30	STL	did not play			
Nov	2	Nyi	2	1	3	0
	4	Bos	0	1	1	0
	7	DET	1	1	2	0
	8	BOS	0	0	0	0
	11	Tor	0	2	2	0
	13	WAS	1	1	2	0
	15	PHI	0	2	2	0
	17	HAR	0	0	0	0
	18	BUF	1	2	3	0
	21	TOR	2	2	4	0
	24	Phi	0	1	1	0
	28	Chi	0	2	2	2
	30	Nyi	1	2	3	2
Dec	5	MIN	0	0	0	0
	7	WIN	0	0	0	0
	9	Har	1	1	2	0
	12	Atl	0	1	1	0
	14	Mon	1	1	2	0
	16	Win	1	1	2	0
	19	Det	2	1	3	0
	21	COL	0	1	1	0
	22	LA	2	1	3	0
	26	Col	1	1	2	0
	28	VAN	1	0	1	0
	30	Que	0	1	1	0
Jan	2	Har	0	1	1	0
	5	La	2	0	2	0
	7	MON	0	0	0	2
	9	QUE	1	0	1	0
	11	Nyr	0	1	1	0
	13	Buf	0	2	2	0
	16	WAS	1	1	2	0
	17	BOS	0	0	0	0
	19	PIT	2	2	4	0
	20	BUF	0	1	1	0
	23	Pit	1	1	2	0
	26	Tor	0	2	2	0
	27	Phi	1	1	2	0
	29	STL	0	0	0	0
	30	LA	1	4	5	0
Feb	1	Win	3	1	4	0
	3	La	1	1	2	0
	6	Stl	1	2	3	2
	8	Atl	1	0	1	2
	10	WIN	0	0	0	0
	13	MIN	0	1	1	0
	15	Was	0	7	7	0
	17	Stl	1	2	3	0
	19	HAR	0	0	0	0
	20	NYR	0	0	0	0
	22	COL	0	0	0	0
	24	Bos	0	1	1	0
	27	CHI	0	2	2	0
	29	Buf	0	1	1	0

DATE		TEAM	G	A	P	Pim
Mar	1	Van	0	0	0	0
	4	NYI	2	2	4	0
	6	MON	1	2	3	0
	8	PIT	1	1	2	0
	9	PHI	0	1	1	0
	12	QUE	2	0	2	2
	14	Chi	0	0	0	5*
	15	Mon	1	0	1	0
	19	Nyr	0	1	1	0
	21	Pit	3	1	4	0
	25	ATL	2	2	4	0
	26	DET	0	2	2	0
	29	TOR	2	4	6	0
Apr	1	VAN	0	0	0	0
	2	Min	1	0	1	0
	4	Col	1	2	3	2
TOTALS			79	51	86	137	21

* fighting major with Doug Lecuyer

1980–81 EDMONTON

DATE		TEAM	G	A	P	Pim
Oct	10	Que	2	1	3	0
	12	Col	0	2	2	0
	15	BUF	0	0	0	0
	18	NYI	2	1	3	0
	19	NYR	1	3	4	0
	22	Cal	0	2	2	0
	24	Min	0	0	0	0
	26	La	0	0	0	0
	29	Tor	0	2	2	0
Nov	1	Was	0	0	0	0
	3	Pit	2	0	2	2
	5	VAN	0	2	2	0
	7	WIN	0	1	1	0
	9	Stl	0	2	2	0
	13	PHI	0	0	0	0
	15	TOR	1	0	1	0
	16	CHI	1	2	3	0
	19	Van	0	2	2	2
	23	Buf	0	1	1	0
	25	COL	0	1	1	0
	26	Chi	1	4	5	0
	28	HAR	0	2	2	0
	29	BOS	1	0	1	0
Dec	5	Nyr	1	0	1	0
	7	Har	1	2	3	12*
	10	Nyi	0	0	0	0
	13	MON	0	1	1	0
	14	QUE	0	1	1	0
	16	DET	0	2	2	0
	17	WAS	0	0	0	0
	20	Mon	0	1	1	0
	23	LA	3	0	3	0
	27	Det	0	3	3	0
	29	Phi	0	0	0	0
	30	CAL	1	1	2	0
Jan	2	Bos	0	1	1	0
	3	Tor	1	2	3	0
	7	Was	2	2	4	2
	9	Har	0	1	1	0
	11	QUE	1	4	5	0
	12	MON	0	0	0	2
	14	TOR	2	1	3	0
	16	BUF	0	0	0	0
	17	STL	1	3	4	0

DATE		TEAM	G	A	P	Pim
	21	Van	1	2	3	0
	23	Nyr	0	2	2	0
	24	MIN	0	1	1	0
	28	Mon	1	4	5	0
	30	Chi	1	2	3	0
Feb	1	WAS	0	2	2	0
	3	STL	0	0	0	2
	4	CHI	1	0	1	0
	6	Win	3	3	6	0
	8	Cal	1	2	3	0
	13	Que	1	0	1	0
	15	Buf	0	1	1	0
	18	Stl	5	2	7	0
	20	Bos	0	0	0	0
	21	WIN	0	1	1	0
	24	LA	1	0	1	0
	25	Phi	2	2	4	0
	27	Det	1	1	2	0
	28	COL	0	1	1	0
Mar	3	NYI	2	2	4	0
	4	NYR	1	0	1	0
	7	PHI	4	0	4	0
	8	PIT	0	1	1	0
	12	Nyi	0	0	0	0
	15	CAL	1	0	1	0
	16	Pit	0	3	3	0
	18	MIN	0	4	4	0
	20	Min	1	0	1	2
	21	La	1	4	5	0
	23	BOS	0	2	2	0
	25	HAR	1	3	4	2
	28	DET	0	1	1	0
	29	PIT	0	3	3	0
Apr	1	Col	0	2	2	0
	3	VAN	1	1	2	2
	4	Win	1	4	5	0
TOTALS			80	55	109	164	28

* minor/misconduct

1981–82 EDMONTON

DATE		TEAM	G	A	P	Pim
Oct	7	Col	0	1	1	0
	9	VAN	0	0	0	4
	10	LA	1	1	2	0
	14	Win	1	0	1	0
	16	Cal	1	2	3	0
	18	CHI	1	3	4	0
	20	CAL	1	1	2	0
	21	Har	0	0	0	0
	23	Pit	1	1	2	0
	24	COL	1	1	2	0
	27	NYI	0	1	1	0
	28	NYR	2	2	4	0
	31	Que	4	1	5	0
Nov	4	Tor	2	0	2	2
	7	Col	0	0	0	0
	11	HAR	2	1	3	0
	12	BOS	0	2	2	0
	14	NYI	1	3	4	0
	15	NYR	1	2	3	0
	17	STL	2	1	3	0
	19	MIN	0	0	0	0
	21	Van	2	2	4	2
	23	Det	1	1	2	0
	25	La	4	1	5	0

DATE		TEAM	G	A	P	Pim
	27	Chi	2	3	5	0
	29	WIN	1	3	4	2
Dec	1	MON	0	3	3	0
	2	QUE	0	2	2	0
	4	Van	0	3	3	0
	5	VAN	0	2	2	2
	9	LA	1	0	1	0
	13	Nyi	1	3	4	0
	16	COL	1	2	3	0
	17	CAL	1	0	1	2
	19	Min	3	4	7	0
	20	Cal	2	1	3	0
	23	Van	1	3	4	0
	27	La	4	1	5	0
	30	Phi	5	1	6	0
	31	VAN	0	0	0	0
Jan	2	Bos	1	1	2	2
	6	Col	2	2	4	0
	9	Cal	1	4	5	0
	10	CAL	0	0	0	0
	13	WAS	1	2	3	0
	14	PHI	1	0	1	0
	16	TOR	1	0	1	0
	17	DET	0	2	2	0
	20	Stl	3	2	5	0
	22	VAN	1	1	2	2
	24	Col	0	3	3	0
	26	STL	1	1	2	0
	27	CHI	1	1	2	2
	29	Buf	1	0	1	0
	31	Phi	3	2	5	0
Feb	3	Mon	1	1	2	0
	6	Tor	0	2	2	0
	7	Nyr	1	1	2	0
	12	Was	1	2	3	0
	14	Bos	0	1	1	0
	17	Min	2	3	5	0
	19	Har	3	2	5	0
	21	DET	1	4	5	0
	24	BUF	3	2	5	0
	27	PIT	1	1	2	0
	28	WAS	2	1	3	0
Mar	2	MON	0	2	2	0
	3	QUE	0	2	2	0
	6	COL	0	0	0	2
	10	LA	0	2	2	0
	12	Buf	0	0	0	0
	13	Van	0	3	3	0
	15	La	0	2	2	2
	17	Pit	3	2	5	0
	19	Cal	1	1	2	0
	25	CAL	2	2	4	2
	26	COL	1	2	3	0
	28	LA	1	1	2	0
	31	La	0	3	3	0
Apr	4	Win	0	1	1	0
TOTALS			80	92	120	212	26

1982–83 EDMONTON

DATE		TEAM	G	A	P	Pim
Oct	5	Cal	0	1	1	0
	8	Nyi	1	1	2	0
	9	VAN	2	1	3	0
	12	CAL	1	2	3	2
	14	HAR	1	2	3	2
	16	BOS	0	2	2	2

DATE		TEAM	G	A	P	Pim
	17	BUF	1	2	3	0
	20	Har	0	1	1	0
	21	Bos	0	1	1	0
	24	WIN	0	3	3	2
	27	Chi	0	2	2	0
	29	La	1	2	3	0
	31	Van	1	0	1	2
Nov	3	Win	1	1	2	2
	5	Nyr	1	1	2	0
	8	QUE	0	4	4	0
	10	PIT	0	3	3	0
	11	NJ	1	0	1	0
	13	PHI	1	0	1	0
	14	NYR	2	2	4	2
	16	NYI	0	1	1	0
	20	Van	0	1	1	0
	21	Que	3	3	6	0
	24	Was	1	1	2	0
	26	WIN	2	2	4	2
	28	DET	0	4	4	0
Dec	1	Phi	0	2	2	10*
	4	Cal	1	3	4	0
	5	La	1	4	5	0
	7	Stl	2	0	2	0
	9	LA	0	0	0	0
	11	MIN	1	2	3	2
	17	Nj	1	3	4	0
	19	Mon	0	1	1	0
	22	Min	1	2	3	7**
	23	LA	1	0	1	0
	26	CAL	0	2	2	0
	29	Chi	0	2	2	0
	31	VAN	2	1	3	0
Jan	1	Win	0	0	0	0
	4	CAN	1	0	1	0
	5	WIN	2	3	5	0
	7	Pit	2	0	2	0
	9	Det	0	2	2	0
	11	STL	0	2	2	0
	12	CHI	2	1	3	0
	15	MIN	1	5	6	0
	18	LA	1	1	2	0
	19	Van	1	3	4	0
	22	VAN	1	0	1	0
	23	La	1	3	4	2
	26	Tor	2	1	3	2
	29	Cal	0	0	0	0
	30	Nyi	0	1	1	0
Feb	3	La	0	1	1	2
	4	Mon	1	4	5	0
	11	Que	1	2	3	0
	14	MON	2	0	2	0
	17	PHI	0	2	2	0
	19	PIT	2	1	3	2
	20	BUF	0	1	1	0
	22	CAL	1	0	1	0
	23	Was	2	1	3	2
	25	Stl	1	0	1	2
	27	Win	0	1	1	0
Mar	1	NJ	1	1	2	0
	2	WAS	1	1	2	0
	5	TOR	2	3	5	0
	6	BOS	1	0	1	2
	8	HAR	3	1	4	0
	11	Nyr	0	0	0	0
	13	Buf	1	2	3	0
	16	Van	1	2	3	0
	19	Det	1	4	5	0
	21	TOR	1	2	3	6
	23	WIN	0	1	1	0
	26	LA	2	1	3	0

DATE		TEAM	G	A	P	Pim
	29	VAN	1	3	4	2
Apr	1	Win	1	3	4	2
	3	Cal	1	1	2	0
TOTALS		80	71	125	196	59

* misconduct
** minor/fighting major with Neal Broten

1983–84 EDMONTON

DATE		TEAM	G	A	P	Pim
Oct	5	Tor	1	1	2	2
	7	WIN	2	1	3	0
	9	Min	1	2	3	0
	12	Det	2	3	5	0
	15	CAL	1	1	2	0
	16	Cal	1	2	3	0
	19	VAN	2	0	2	0
	20	LA	1	0	1	0
	22	Van	0	3	3	2
	26	TOR	1	0	1	0
	29	MON	0	1	1	0
	30	NYR	1	0	1	0
Nov	2	Was	2	3	5	0
	5	Pit	0	3	3	0
	6	WIN	4	3	7	0
	8	QUE	1	1	2	0
	9	WAS	1	3	4	0
	12	DET	3	2	5	0
	13	CHI	0	1	1	0
	18	Buf	0	3	3	0
	19	Nj	3	5	8	2
	21	Win	1	0	1	2
	23	LA	0	2	2	0
	25	MIN	1	0	1	0
	26	STL	0	5	5	0
	30	Phi	1	1	2	2
Dec	3	La	0	3	3	0
	4	Nyi	0	1	1	0
	7	Van	0	2	2	0
	10	VAN	0	1	1	0
	13	NYI	1	1	2	0
	14	NYR	3	2	5	0
	17	Que	1	5	6	0
	18	WIN	2	2	4	2
	21	Win	3	2	5	0
	23	Cal	1	1	2	0
	26	CAL	1	2	3	2
	28	VAN	0	2	2	0
	30	Bos	0	1	1	2
Jan	3	CAL	1	3	4	0
	4	Min	4	4	8	0
	7	Har	3	0	3	0
	9	DET	2	1	3	2
	11	CHI	1	0	1	0
	13	BUF	0	1	1	0
	15	NJ	0	3	3	0
	18	Van	3	2	5	0
	20	La	2	3	5	0
	21	LA	0	2	2	0
	25	VAN	2	2	4	0
	27	Nj	1	0	1	0
	28	La	0	0	0	0
Feb	3	CAL	did not play			
	5	WAS	did not play			
	7	NYI	did not play			
	9	PHI	did not play			
	11	BOS	did not play			
	12	HAR	did not play			
	15	Win	2	2	4	2

DATE		TEAM	G	A	P	Pim
	17	Bos	0	1	1	2
	19	Pit	2	1	3	0
	21	STL	4	1	5	0
	22	PIT	4	1	5	2
	24	Cal	0	0	0	4
	25	Tor	2	0	2	0
	27	WIN	1	1	2	0
	29	Phi	0	2	2	0
Mar	4	Mon	2	1	3	0
	7	Chi	0	3	3	7*
	10	Nyr	1	0	1	0
	11	Van	2	3	5	0
	13	QUE	1	1	2	0
	15	MON	0	1	1	0
	17	La	1	2	3	0
	18	Buf	0	0	0	0
	21	Har	0	1	1	2
	24	Stl	1	0	1	2
	25	Win	1	0	1	0
	27	CAL	2	2	4	0
	31	LA	0	3	3	0
TOTALS		74	87	118	205	39

* minor/fighting major with Bob Murray

1984–85 EDMONTON

DATE		TEAM	G	A	P	Pim
Oct	11	LA	0	1	1	0
	12	Stl	0	1	1	0
	14	Que	1	3	4	0
	16	Bos	2	1	3	2
	18	MIN	3	0	3	0
	19	WIN	2	3	5	0
	21	Cal	2	2	4	0
	24	Was	0	2	2	0
	26	La	0	4	4	0
	30	Van	1	2	3	2
Nov	2	Chi	0	1	1	0
	4	WIN	1	1	2	0
	6	PIT	1	0	1	0
	8	NJ	0	3	3	2
	9	WAS	2	4	6	0
	11	PHI	2	2	4	0
	14	Mon	0	0	0	0
	15	CAL	1	0	1	0
	17	Van	0	3	3	0
	21	Win	1	2	3	2
	24	Stl	2	3	5	0
	27	TOR	3	2	5	0
	29	BOS	0	2	2	0
	30	HAR	0	2	2	2
Dec	5	Nyi	1	4	5	2
	7	Min	1	2	3	4
	8	VAN	0	0	0	0
	13	LA	1	1	2	0
	15	STL	5	1	6	0
	17	NJ	0	1	1	0
	19	La	2	4	6	0
	21	Van	0	0	0	0
	22	Cal	2	2	4	0
	26	CAL	0	4	4	0
	29	Det	3	3	6	0
	30	VAN	1	2	3	0
Jan	2	Phi	0	0	0	0
	4	Win	0	3	3	0
	6	WIN	1	0	1	0
	8	QUE	1	2	3	2
	10	MON	1	2	3	0
	12	PIT	0	3	3	0

DATE		TEAM	G	A	P	Pim
	13	BUF	1	2	3	0
	16	Nyi	1	1	2	0
	18	VAN	1	0	1	0
	19	Van	1	3	4	4
	21	La	1	1	2	2
	25	Nj	1	2	3	0
	26	Pit	3	1	4	0
	28	Cal	1	2	3	0
	29	CAL	0	2	2	0
Feb	2	Nyr	0	0	0	0
	3	Har	1	2	3	0
	6	WIN	0	1	1	0
	8	MIN	0	2	2	0
	9	DET	0	2	2	0
	15	NYR	2	2	4	2
	16	PHI	0	2	2	0
	18	BUF	2	1	3	0
	19	TOR	2	3	5	0
	22	Que	1	1	2	0
	23	Was	0	1	1	2
	27	Mon	1	0	1	0
Mar	1	La	0	3	3	6
	3	Win	1	1	2	0
	5	CAL	0	1	1	2
	9	Nyr	1	0	1	0
	10	VAN	0	1	1	0
	13	Det	1	4	5	0
	15	Buf	0	1	1	2
	17	LA	0	1	1	2
	20	Chi	0	2	2	0
	22	Tor	0	1	1	0
	26	NYI	1	1	2	0
	28	BOS	0	1	1	0
	29	HAR	1	2	3	0
	31	CHI	1	4	5	0
Apr	2	LA	3	1	4	0
	5	Cal	1	1	2	2
	6	Win	0	2	2	10*
TOTALS		80	73	135	208	52

* misconduct

1985–86 EDMONTON

DATE		TEAM	G	A	P	Pim
Oct	10	Win	2	1	3	2
	13	Stl	0	2	2	0
	16	Nyi	0	1	1	0
	18	Bos	0	2	2	0
	20	LA	1	2	3	0
	23	WIN	0	1	1	0
	25	Cal	1	2	3	2
	28	CAL	1	4	5	0
	30	Win	0	4	4	0
Nov	1	Buf	0	0	0	0
	3	Tor	3	0	3	2
	5	VAN	2	1	3	0
	6	LA	1	1	2	2
	8	Van	0	4	4	0
	12	WAS	1	0	1	0
	14	PHI	0	1	1	0
	16	NYI	1	0	1	0
	17	NYR	0	2	2	0
	19	QUE	1	1	2	2
	20	MON	0	1	1	0
	23	Nj	0	1	1	0
	27	Van	2	0	2	0
	30	Har	1	3	4	0
Dec	1	Cal	0	1	1	0
	3	LA	0	1	1	2

DATE	TEAM	G	A	P	Pim
5	La	0	5	5	2
7	Min	1	4	5	0
8	Chi	0	1	1	0
10	STL	0	2	2	0
11	CHI	0	7	7	0
13	WIN	2	2	4	12*
15	Van	0	3	3	2
18	Was	0	1	1	0
20	La	0	6	6	0
22	Win	2	1	3	0
29	VAN	0	2	2	0
31	Phi	3	0	3	0
Jan 2	CAL	1	1	2	0
4	Har	0	2	2	0
5	Cal	1	2	3	0
8	TOR	3	3	6	0
10	QUE	0	3	3	0
11	MON	1	3	4	0
13	BOS	1	2	3	2
15	HAR	2	1	3	0
18	Nyr	0	2	2	0
22	Pit	1	1	2	0
24	Nj	1	3	4	0
25	La	1	1	2	0
27	CHI	0	0	0	0
29	STL	0	3	3	0
31	Cal	0	4	4	0
Feb 1	CAL	0	3	3	0
6	NJ	0	3	3	0
8	WAS	0	2	2	0
9	BUF	0	1	1	0
11	DET	0	1	1	0
14	Que	0	7	7	2
16	Buf	1	3	4	0
19	Tor	2	0	2	0
22	Bos	1	1	2	0
24	Mon	1	1	2	2
26	WIN	2	4	6	0
Mar 2	Phi	0	1	1	0
4	VAN	0	4	4	0
5	La	2	2	4	2
7	Pit	0	2	2	0
9	LA	1	3	4	4
11	MIN	0	0	0	0
12	WIN	0	2	2	0
14	Det	1	4	5	2
18	Win	1	2	3	2
21	Win	0	1	1	0
25	DET	0	3	3	0
26	PIT	1	3	4	0
28	NYR	0	1	1	2
29	NYI	0	3	3	0
Apr 2	Van	1	1	2	0
4	CAL	0	3	3	0
6	VAN	0	1	1	0
TOTALS	80	52	163	215	46

* minor/misconduct

1986–87 EDMONTON

DATE	TEAM	G	A	P	Pim
Oct 9	PHI	0	0	0	0
11	MON	2	2	4	2
12	WIN	1	0	1	0
15	Que	0	5	5	0
17	Det	0	4	4	2
19	LA	0	2	2	0
21	Chi	2	3	5	0
22	CAL	0	1	1	0
24	Bos	3	1	4	0
26	Van	0	2	2	0
29	Was	1	1	2	0
31	VAN	2	1	3	0
Nov 2	La	0	3	3	0
5	Cal	1	0	1	0
7	CAL	1	1	2	0
8	Mon	0	0	0	0
11	NYI	0	1	1	0
13	BOS	1	0	1	0
15	HAR	0	1	1	0
16	NYR	1	2	3	0
19	Nyr	1	0	1	0
22	Van	3	2	5	2
24	CAL	1	1	2	2
26	Win	1	2	3	0
28	Chi	0	2	2	0
Dec 3	Nyi	1	2	3	0
5	PIT	0	3	3	0
7	PHI	1	0	1	0
9	MIN	1	1	2	2
10	WIN	3	0	3	2
12	Win	0	3	3	0
14	LA	0	2	2	0
17	Que	4	1	5	0
19	Van	2	0	2	0
20	La	2	3	5	0
23	Win	0	0	0	2
28	Phi	2	1	3	0
30	VAN	2	2	4	0
Jan 3	LA	1	2	3	0
7	La	0	1	1	0
9	Stl	0	0	0	0
11	Cal	0	2	2	0
13	DET	1	2	3	0
15	QUE	1	1	2	0
17	TOR	1	3	4	0
18	BUF	0	2	2	0
21	WIN	2	1	3	0
23	Nyr	2	2	4	0
24	Pit	1	3	4	2
27	VAN	0	2	2	0
28	Van	0	4	4	2
30	Min	1	0	1	0
Feb 1	CHI	0	2	2	0
3	STL	0	1	1	0
4	MIN	1	3	4	2
6	Nyi	0	2	2	0
8	Stl	2	2	4	0
15	Was	0	0	0	0
18	Tor	1	4	5	0
22	WIN	1	1	2	0
24	PIT	0	1	1	2
25	NJ	0	0	0	0
27	WAS	0	0	0	0
Mar 4	VAN	1	2	3	0
6	La	1	4	5	0
7	Mon	0	2	2	0
11	Det	1	3	4	0
14	Buf	2	1	3	2
15	Har	1	1	2	0
17	Nj	0	3	3	0
19	CAL	1	2	3	0
20	Cal	0	1	1	2
23	NJ	0	3	3	0
25	HAR	0	2	2	0
26	BOS	0	0	0	2
28	TOR	0	0	0	0
29	BUF	0	0	0	0
31	Win	0	1	1	0
Apr 2	Cal	1	0	1	0
4	LA	did not play			
TOTALS	79	62	121	183	28

1987–88 EDMONTON

DATE	TEAM	G	A	P	Pim
Oct 9	Det	0	1	1	0
11	LA	1	4	5	0
14	Cal	1	1	2	0
16	CAL	0	1	1	0
17	Bos	1	2	3	0
21	La	2	1	3	0
23	VAN	0	2	2	0
24	Van	2	3	5	2
27	QUE	0	0	0	0
28	MON	0	1	1	0
31	NJ	0	3	3	0
Nov 1	NYR	0	2	2	0
4	Nyr	3	2	5	0
5	CAL	1	2	3	0
7	Buf	0	2	2	0
10	LA	0	1	1	4
14	STL	0	4	4	0
15	CHI	1	2	3	0
18	Que	0	2	2	0
20	Pit	0	2	2	0
22	WIN	2	0	2	2
25	Nj	1	3	4	0
27	Chi	1	1	2	2
29	BUF	0	2	2	0
Dec 1	WAS	0	0	0	0
2	DET	0	1	1	0
5	Tor	2	0	2	0
6	Min	5	1	6	0
9	Win	0	1	1	0
11	Van	0	1	1	2
12	VAN	2	1	3	0
16	LA	1	1	2	0
18	Win	0	2	2	0
19	Har	0	0	0	0
22	La	0	2	2	2
26	CAL	1	0	1	0
28	Van	0	1	1	0
30	Phi	1	3	4	0
Jan 2	WAS	did not play			
4	BOS	did not play			
6	HAR	did not play			
8	WIN	did not play			
9	Nyi	did not play			
11	Was	did not play			
13	Cal	did not play			
15	Win	did not play			
18	MON	did not play			
19	QUE	did not play			
21	PHI	did not play			
23	NYI	did not play			
25	PIT	did not play			
29	Cal	0	4	4	0
30	Har	1	2	3	0
Feb 3	Nj	1	2	3	2
6	LA	1	1	2	2
11	VAN	1	2	3	0
12	Bos	0	2	2	0
14	Van	0	1	1	0
17	Tor	0	2	2	0
19	Pit	0	0	0	0
21	WIN	did not play			
23	STL	did not play			
24	CHI	did not play			
28	Cal	1	0	1	2

DATE	TEAM	G	A	P	Pim
Mar 1	La	1	1	2	2
4	Phi	0	5	5	0
5	CAL	0	3	3	0
7	WIN	0	5	5	0
9	Mon	0	0	0	0
12	VAN	0	2	2	0
15	Buf	0	3	3	0
18	Win	0	1	1	0
20	MIN	1	2	3	0
22	DET	0	3	3	0
24	NYR	0	0	0	0
26	NYI	1	2	3	0
28	TOR	1	3	4	0
30	Min	1	3	4	2
Apr 1	Stl	0	3	3	0
3	La	0	1	1	0
TOTALS	64	40	109	149	24

1988–89 LOS ANGELES

DATE	TEAM	G	A	P	Pim
Oct 6	Det	1	3	4	0
8	Cal	2	2	4	0
9	Nyi	1	1	2	0
12	Bos	2	0	2	0
15	Phi	0	1	1	0
17	CAL	1	1	2	0
19	EDM	0	2	2	0
22	Min	0	2	2	0
25	Edm	0	2	2	0
28	WIN	0	2	2	0
30	WIN	1	0	1	0
Nov 1	QUE	1	0	1	0
2	MON	0	3	3	0
5	TOR	0	2	2	0
6	CHI	2	1	3	0
10	Har	0	2	2	2
12	Pit	0	1	1	0
15	Van	2	0	2	2
17	Nyr	0	3	3	2
19	Buf	1	0	1	0
22	PHI	0	2	2	0
23	DET	1	5	6	0
26	CAL	1	0	1	0
27	VAN	0	0	0	4
29	Nj	2	2	4	0
Dec 1	Har	0	5	5	2
3	Chi	1	3	4	0
6	Win	1	1	2	0
8	Win	1	3	4	0
10	NYI	0	1	1	0
12	NYR	1	0	1	0
14	PIT	did not play			
16	DET	1	2	3	2
17	MIN	0	0	0	0
20	Cal	0	2	2	0
21	Min	1	0	1	0
23	VAN	2	2	4	0
27	Mon	0	1	1	2
29	Van	1	2	3	0
Jan 5	CAL	0	2	2	0
6	WIN	0	0	0	0
8	WIN	1	0	1	0
10	Edm	0	4	4	2
12	Stl	1	0	1	0
14	Har	2	1	3	0
17	STL	0	0	0	0
19	NYI	0	1	1	0
21	HAR	1	3	4	2
24	WAS	0	2	2	0

DATE		TEAM	G	A	P	Pim
	26	Van	0	1	1	0
	28	Edm	0	3	3	0
	31	Cal	1	3	4	0
Feb	2	Nj	1	0	1	0
	4	Buf	3	1	4	0
	9	BOS	0	0	0	0
	10	WAS	1	2	3	0
	12	CHI	3	0	3	0
	15	Bos	0	1	1	0
	18	Que	2	5	7	0
	20	Tor	2	1	3	0
	22	Was	0	1	1	0
	24	EDM	0	0	0	0
	26	NJ	0	0	0	0
	27	NYR	0	3	3	0
Mar	1	BUF	1	1	2	0
	2	STL	1	1	2	0
	4	Phi	2	4	6	0
	7	Pit	0	2	2	0
	10	VAN	1	0	1	2
	12	EDM	1	1	2	0
	14	QUE	0	1	1	2
	15	MON	0	1	1	0
	18	Cal	0	2	2	2
	21	EDM	0	2	2	0
	23	CAL	0	1	1	0
	25	Edm	0	1	1	0
	28	Win	1	2	3	0
	29	Win	1	0	1	0
Apr	1	Van	0	3	3	0
	2	VAN	did not play			
TOTALS		78	54	114	168	26

1989–90 LOS ANGELES

DATE		TEAM	G	A	P	Pim
Oct	5	Tor	0	1	1	0
	7	Edm	2	0	2	0
	8	Det	0	3	3	0
	11	Nyi	1	2	3	0
	13	VAN	0	3	3	0
	15	EDM	2	1	3	0
	17	Bos	0	0	0	0
	21	STL	1	0	1	0
	22	CHI	0	2	2	0
	25	Cal	0	0	0	0
	27	WIN	0	2	2	0
	29	WIN	0	0	0	2
	31	PIT	3	3	6	0
Nov	2	BOS	0	0	0	0
	4	HAR	0	1	1	20*
	5	BUF	0	2	2	0
	8	Cal	1	2	3	0
	11	Mon	0	3	3	0
	14	CAL	0	4	4	0
	15	EDM	0	1	1	0
	18	Was	0	2	2	2
	22	Chi	1	2	3	0
	25	Van	0	2	2	0
	26	VAN	0	3	3	0
	30	Edm	1	1	2	2
Dec	2	Nyr	0	3	3	0
	6	Van	0	2	2	0
	8	EDM	1	1	2	2
	10	QUE	0	4	4	0
	11	MON	0	1	1	0
	13	HAR	1	1	2	0
	15	NJ	1	0	1	0
	16	PHI	0	0	0	0
	19	Win	2	4	6	0

DATE		TEAM	G	A	P	Pim
	21	Que	1	1	2	0
	23	Van	0	1	1	0
	27	Cal	1	1	2	2
	30	Phi	0	2	2	0
Jan	1	WAS	2	1	3	4
	2	NYI	0	2	2	0
	4	NJ	0	1	1	0
	6	TOR	1	1	2	0
	9	Stl	1	0	1	0
	11	Edm	1	0	1	2
	13	Har	0	2	2	0
	16	Buf	1	1	2	0
	18	Det	2	2	4	0
	23	VAN	0	0	0	0
	25	EDM	0	0	0	2
	27	Nyr	1	0	1	0
	30	Nj	0	2	2	0
Feb	1	Chi	1	1	2	2
	3	Cal	0	2	2	0
	6	CAL	0	1	1	0
	8	Win	0	0	0	0
	10	PIT	0	1	1	0
	12	TOR	0	0	0	0
	14	DET	2	1	3	0
	15	MIN	0	1	1	2
	17	Que	2	3	5	0
	19	Was	1	0	1	0
	21	Min	1	2	3	0
	24	Van	0	2	2	0
	28	Edm	1	2	3	0
Mar	2	WIN	0	2	2	0
	4	WIN	0	1	1	0
	5	CAL	0	0	0	0
	7	Mon	1	1	2	0
	10	Pit	1	2	3	0
	12	NYR	0	2	2	0
	14	BUF	1	2	3	0
	17	BOS	1	2	3	0
	18	PHI	did not play			
	20	MIN	did not play			
	22	Nyi	0	1	1	0
	24	Stl	did not play			
	27	Win	did not play			
	29	Win	did not play			
	31	VAN	did not play			
Apr	1	CAL	did not play			
Totals		73	40	102	142	42

* misconduct/game misconduct

1990–91 LOS ANGELES

DATE		TEAM	G	A	P	Pim
Oct	4	Nyi	2	1	3	0
	6	Van	0	0	0	0
	9	VAN	0	1	1	0
	11	Edm	1	4	5	0
	13	Bos	2	2	4	0
	14	Stl	0	1	1	0
	17	Min	1	2	3	0
	19	Har	1	0	1	0
	23	Cal	0	2	2	0
	26	WIN	0	1	1	0
	28	WIN	0	2	2	0
	30	NYI	1	1	2	0
	31	NYR	1	0	1	0
Nov	2	WAS	1	1	2	0
	4	CHI	0	1	1	0
	8	Det	1	1	2	0
	10	Edm	1	1	2	0

DATE		TEAM	G	A	P	Pim
	14	Buf	1	1	2	0
	17	Pit	0	0	0	0
	20	Nj	1	2	3	0
	22	CAL	0	2	2	0
	24	MON	0	3	3	0
	25	QUE	1	1	2	0
	27	DET	0	1	1	0
	29	STL	1	1	2	0
Dec	1	Tor	0	1	1	0
	5	Win	1	1	2	0
	8	Win	0	2	2	2
	11	Nyr	2	0	2	0
	13	Cal	0	0	0	0
	15	Edm	1	4	5	0
	18	EDM	0	1	1	0
	20	CAL	1	1	2	0
	22	VAN	0	2	2	0
	27	Phi	0	2	2	0
	29	Mon	1	0	1	0
	31	MIN	0	2	2	0
Jan	2	NYR	0	0	0	0
	3	NYI	3	0	3	0
	5	TOR	0	2	2	0
	6	CHI	0	1	1	2
	8	Har	0	2	2	0
	10	Buf	0	4	4	0
	12	Van	1	1	2	2
	14	NJ	1	2	3	0
	16	HAR	0	2	2	4
	17	BOS	1	1	2	0
	22	EDM	did not play			
	25	VAN	1	1	2	0
	26	Van	3	2	5	2
	30	Nj	0	2	2	0
Feb	2	Van	1	2	3	0
	4	DET	0	3	3	0
	5	PHI	0	0	0	0
	8	BUF	0	1	1	0
	9	STL	0	1	1	0
	12	Cal	0	2	2	0
	14	EDM	0	2	2	0
	16	Bos	0	1	1	0
	18	Was	1	2	3	0
	20	Que	1	1	2	0
	22	WIN	1	4	5	0
	24	WIN	1	2	3	0
	26	Pit	0	3	3	0
	28	Win	0	1	1	0
Mar	2	Win	0	3	3	2
	5	WAS	0	3	3	0
	7	PIT	1	1	2	2
	9	QUE	0	2	2	0
	10	MON	0	3	3	0
	12	Phi	0	3	3	0
	14	Chi	0	1	1	0
	16	CAL	0	2	2	0
	17	VAN	0	2	2	0
	20	Tor	0	4	4	0
	23	Cal	0	3	3	0
	24	EDM	0	1	1	0
	26	Edm	2	0	2	0
	28	Min	1	1	2	0
	31	CAL	did not play			
TOTALS		78	41	122	163	16

1991–92 LOS ANGELES

DATE		TEAM	G	A	P	Pim
Oct	4	WIN	0	2	2	0
	6	EDM	0	0	0	0

DATE		TEAM	G	A	P	Pim
	8	Edm	0	1	1	0
	10	Cal	0	0	0	0
	12	Win	0	2	2	0
	16	Sj	did not play			
	19	Min	did not play			
	22	NJ	did not play			
	23	NYR	did not play			
	26	NYI	did not play			
	28	DET	0	1	1	0
	30	HAR	1	1	2	2
	31	BOS	1	1	2	2
Nov	2	TOR	2	2	4	0
	7	Van	0	0	0	2
	9	Edm	0	2	2	0
	11	WIN	0	0	0	0
	12	VAN	1	0	1	0
	14	Buf	0	0	0	0
	16	Det	0	0	0	0
	19	SJ	0	2	2	0
	21	Nyr	1	0	1	2
	23	Sj	3	1	4	0
	26	Tor	1	3	4	0
	28	CAL	0	3	3	0
	30	Nj	0	1	1	0
Dec	3	SJ	1	1	2	0
	5	CHI	0	2	2	0
	7	QUE	0	2	2	0
	12	Win	1	0	1	0
	14	Van	1	2	3	0
	17	Min	0	1	1	0
	21	Det	1	0	1	0
	26	Sj	1	2	3	0
	28	EDM	1	3	4	0
	29	CAL	0	0	0	0
	31	Van	0	1	1	12*
Jan	2	Edm	0	0	0	0
	4	Phi	1	2	3	0
	7	PIT	0	1	1	0
	9	PHI	1	0	1	0
	10	WAS	0	2	2	0
	12	NJ	0	2	2	0
	14	Sj	0	1	1	0
	16	Was	0	1	1	0
	22	MIN	0	0	0	0
	23	STL	0	2	2	0
	25	Cal	0	2	2	0
	28	Stl	1	1	2	0
	30	Nyr	0	0	0	0
Feb	1	Chi	1	1	2	0
	4	Nyi	0	1	1	0
	6	Har	0	3	3	0
	8	PIT	2	0	2	0
	9	BUF	0	1	1	0
	11	STL	0	1	1	0
	13	CHI	0	0	0	0
	15	Was	0	3	3	0
	17	Bos	2	2	4	0
	19	EDM	1	1	2	0
	21	CAL	1	2	3	0
	23	WIN	0	3	3	0
	25	VAN	0	1	1	0
	27	Que	did not play			
	29	Mon	1	3	4	0
Mar	3	Phi	0	1	1	0
	4	SJ	0	3	3	0
	7	Pit	1	2	3	0
	9	Tor	0	1	1	0
	11	HAR	0	0	0	0
	14	MON	0	1	1	0
	15	BOS	0	1	1	0
	17	Win	0	1	1	0

DATE	TEAM	G	A	P	Pim
19	Buf	0	0	0	0
21	Cal	2	1	3	0
26	CAL	1	0	1	0
27	WIN	0	3	3	0
29	EDM	0	0	0	0
Apr 2	VAN	0	4	4	12*
4	Van	0	0	0	0
TOTALS	74	31	90	121	34

* minor/misconduct

1992–93 LOS ANGELES

DATE	TEAM	G	A	P	Pim
Oct 6	CAL	did not play			
8	Det	did not play			
10	Win	did not play			
12	Sj	did not play			
15	Cal	did not play			
17	Bos	did not play			
20	CAL	did not play			
23	WIN	did not play			
24	MIN	did not play			
27	NYI	did not play			
29	BOS	did not play			
31	IIAR	did not play			
Nov 5	Nj	did not play			
7	Buf	did not play			
8	SJ	did not play			
10	WIN	did not play			
12	Van	did not play			
14	Edm	did not play			
16	VAN	did not play			
17	SJ	did not play			
19	Chi	did not play			
21	Tor	did not play			
25	EDM	did not play			
27	DET	did not play			
28	TOR	did not play			
Dec 1	CHI*	did not play			
3	Pit	did not play			
5	Har	did not play			
8	Mon+	did not play			
10	Que	did not play			
12	Stl	did not play			
15	Tb	did not play			
18	EDM	did not play			
19	CAL	did not play			
22	Van	did not play			
26	SJ	did not play			
29	Phi	did not play			
31	VAN	did not play			
Jan 2	Mon	did not play			
6	Tb	0	2	2	0
8	WIN	2	0	2	0
10	CHI	0	2	2	0
12	OTT	0	1	1	0
14	NJ	0	0	0	0
16	Win	0	1	1	0
19	EDM	0	1	1	0
21	Van	0	2	2	0
23	Nyr	0	0	0	0
26	Sj	0	2	2	0
28	Cal	0	1	1	0
30	Chi	0	0	0	0
Feb 2	QUE	0	0	0	0
3	MON	0	0	0	0
9	Edm	0	2	2	0
11	Det	0	2	2	0
13	Was	0	0	0	0

DATE	TEAM	G	A	P	Pim
15	Van	0	1	1	0
16	MIN	1	4	5	0
18	CHI	0	0	0	0
20	WAS	0	1	1	0
22	TB	1	3	4	2
25	STL	0	0	0	0
27	Tor	0	0	0	0
Mar 2	Cal	2	0	2	0
4	Ott	0	4	4	2
6	Edm	1	2	3	0
9	NYR	0	2	2	0
11	PIT	1	1	2	0
15	BUF	1	2	3	0
16	Win	1	2	3	0
18	Nyi	1	0	1	0
20	Stl	0	1	1	2
24	VAN	0	2	2	0
26	EDM	1	0	1	0
28	WIN	0	0	0	0
29	DET	2	2	4	0
31	TOR	0	2	2	0
Apr 1	PHI	0	2	2	0
3	Min	0	0	0	0
6	Cal	0	0	0	0
8	Sj	0	1	1	0
10	SJ	1	1	2	0
13	VAN	0	0	0	0
15	Van	1	2	3	0
TOTALS	45	16	49	65	6

* played at Milwaukee
+ played at Phoenix

1993–94 LOS ANGELES

DATE	TEAM	G	A	P	Pim
Oct 6	Van	0	0	0	0
9	Det	2	4	6	0
10	Sj	0	2	2	0
12	Nyi	1	2	3	2
14	Edm	0	2	2	0
16	Cal	1	3	4	0
19	FLO	0	0	0	2
20	TB	1	2	3	0
22	WAS	1	1	2	2
24	NYR	1	1	2	0
26	NYI	0	0	0	0
27	DET	0	2	2	0
29	WIN	1	2	3	0
Nov 3	Nj	1	1	2	0
6	Pit	0	4	4	0
9	CAL	0	1	1	0
10	VAN	0	0	0	2
13	Stl	0	2	2	0
18	Tor	0	1	1	0
20	STL	0	1	1	0
21	DAL	0	1	1	0
25	QUE	1	3	4	0
27	MON	0	0	0	0
30	Win	2	2	4	0
Dec 2	Ana	0	2	2	0
4	Tb	0	0	0	0
8	Flo	0	2	2	2
11	Stl	0	2	2	0
13	OTT	1	1	2	0
14	PIT	0	0	0	0
17	BUF	0	0	0	0
18	TOR	0	0	0	0
20	CAL	2	0	2	0
23	Dal	0	0	0	0

DATE	TEAM	G	A	P	Pim
26	ANA	0	0	0	0
28	Van	1	2	3	2
31	DET	0	1	1	0
Jan 1	TOR	1	2	3	0
4	Que	0	4	4	0
8	Det	0	0	0	0
11	SJ	0	1	1	0
12	Har	2	2	4	0
15	NJ	2	1	3	0
16	PHI	1	1	2	0
18	DAL	0	2	2	0
24	CAL*	1	2	3	0
25	Win	0	2	2	0
27	Nyr	1	0	1	0
29	Ana	0	1	1	2
31	VAN	0	0	0	0
Feb 2	EDM	1	0	1	0
5	Cal	1	1	2	0
9	Chi	0	1	1	0
11	ANA	2	3	5	0
12	Was	0	0	0	0
14	Bos	0	2	2	0
18	Phi	0	1	1	2
19	SJ	0	2	2	0
21	Tor	2	0	2	0
23	Dal	0	0	0	0
25	EDM	1	0	1	0
26	CAL	1	0	1	0
28	Mon	0	1	1	0
Mar 2	HAR	1	1	2	0
3	BOS	0	1	1	0
6	CHI	0	0	0	0
9	Chi	0	0	0	0
12	Buf	0	0	0	0
15	Ott	1	3	4	0
16	ANA	0	0	0	0
19	Sj	0	2	2	0
20	SJ	2	0	2	0
23	Van	1	0	1	2
25	EDM	0	1	1	0
27	VAN	0	2	2	0
30	Ana	0	0	0	2
Apr 2	Edm	1	1	2	0
3	Edm+	0	3	3	0
5	Sj	0	1	1	0
7	STL	0	0	0	0
9	WIN	0	1	1	0
10	CHI	did not play			
13	Cal	did not play			
14	Edm	did not play			
TOTALS	81	38	92	130	20

* played at Phoenix
+ played at Sacramento

1994–95 LOS ANGELES

DATE	TEAM	G	A	P	Pim
Jan 20	Tor	1	1	2	2
22	Edm	0	2	2	0
24	Dal	0	1	1	0
26	STL	1	0	1	0
28	Win	0	0	0	0
29	Chi	0	1	1	0
Feb 4	Det	0	1	1	0
5	Ana	0	1	1	0
7	STL	0	1	1	0
11	TOR	0	1	1	0
12	DET	0	1	1	0
15	DAL	0	0	0	0

DATE	TEAM	G	A	P	Pim
17	Sj	0	0	0	0
18	Van	1	1	2	0
20	VAN	0	1	1	0
23	Cal	1	1	2	0
25	EDM	0	0	0	0
28	Chi	0	0	0	0
Mar 4	Van	0	1	1	0
6	DAL	0	1	1	0
9	CHI	0	0	0	0
11	WIN	0	0	0	0
13	TOR	1	1	2	0
14	DET	0	0	0	0
16	Stl	0	0	0	0
18	Tor	0	2	2	0
20	Stl	2	1	3	0
21	ANA	0	2	2	0
25	Sj	0	0	0	0
26	SJ	0	2	2	0
28	CAL	0	3	3	0
29	VAN	0	0	0	0
Apr 1	Win	2	0	2	0
3	Edm	0	2	2	2
6	Dal	1	0	1	0
7	CAL	0	2	2	0
9	ANA	0	1	1	2
12	Cal	0	0	0	0
16	SJ	0	0	0	0
17	CAL	0	1	1	0
19	EDM	0	0	0	0
21	Edm	0	1	1	0
23	Ana	0	1	1	0
25	Det	0	1	1	0
28	SJ	0	0	0	0
30	Ana	1	1	2	0
May 2	WIN	0	0	0	0
3	CHI	0	1	1	0
TOTALS	48	11	37	48	6

1995–96 LOS ANGELES/ST. LOUIS

DATE	TEAM	G	A	P	Pim
Oct 7	Col	0	2	2	0
10	Chi	0	1	1	0
12	Van	1	3	4	0
15	VAN	0	0	0	0
18	Phi	0	0	0	0
20	WAS	0	4	4	2
21	PIT	0	1	1	2
23	MON	0	0	0	2
26	OTT	0	1	1	10*
28	TOR	1	1	2	0
31	Cal	0	0	0	0
Nov 2	Nyr	1	1	2	0
4	Nj	0	1	1	0
7	STL	0	1	1	0
8	DAL	0	2	2	0
11	Pit	1	1	2	0
13	ANA	1	2	3	0
14	Det	1	1	2	0
16	Nyi	1	5	6	0
18	Flo	0	0	0	0
21	PHI	0	0	0	0
22	NYI	0	2	2	0
24	BOS	0	0	0	0
26	FLO	0	0	0	0
27	TB	0	0	0	0
30	Was	0	1	1	12**
Dec 2	Dal	0	0	0	0
6	Win	1	2	3	0
9	Stl	0	0	0	0

150   THE GREAT ONE

DATE	TEAM	G	A	P	Pim
11	CAL	0	1	1	0
13	Ott	0	2	2	0
16	Tor	0	3	3	0
20	Van	1	0	1	2
22	SJ	0	0	0	0
23	Col	0	0	0	0
27	Ana	0	2	2	0
29	EDM	1	0	1	0
31	ANA	0	0	0	0
Jan 3	Win	1	2	3	0
5	SJ	1	3	4	0
6	Sj	1	2	3	0
8	DAL	0	2	2	0
10	TOR	0	1	1	0
12	DET	0	1	1	0
14	CHI	0	1	1	0
16	Cal	0	2	2	0
22	NYR	0	0	0	0
23	NJ	0	0	0	0
25	HAR	0	1	1	0
27	Ana	1	3	4	0
31	Har	0	3	3	0
Feb 1	SJ	0	1	1	0
3	CAL	0	0	0	0
6	Chi	0	0	0	0
8	Tor	0	1	1	0
10	Sj	0	0	0	0
13	DET	0	0	0	2
14	BUF	did not play			
17	Ana	did not play			
19	Bos	0	1	1	0
21	EDM	1	0	1	0
23	COL	0	1	1	0
24	STL	0	0	0	0
26	WIN	0	1	1	0
	TRADED				
Feb 29	VAN	1	0	1	0
Mar 3	EDM	0	1	1	0
5	Flo	0	0	0	0
7	Cal	0	2	2	0
9	Har	2	1	3	0
12	CAL	0	0	0	2
15	SJ	1	2	3	0
17	ANA	0	1	1	0
18	LA	1	1	2	0
20	DAL	0	1	1	0
22	Ana	0	0	0	0
24	Det	1	0	1	0
26	PIT	0	1	1	0
28	Nj	1	2	3	0
31	DET	0	0	0	0
Apr 3	COL	1	1	2	0
4	Tor	0	0	0	0
6	TOR	did not play			
8	Win	did not play			
11	Col	did not play			
14	CHI	0	0	0	0
TOTALS	62	15	66	81	32
	18	8	13	21	2
	80	23	79	102	34

* misconduct
** minor/misconduct

1996–97 RANGERS

DATE	TEAM	G	A	P	Pim
Oct 5	BOS	0	0	0	0
6	Flo	0	1	1	0
8	FLO	0	1	1	0
10	Dal	1	0	1	0
12	MON	0	1	1	0
14	Cal	1	1	2	0
16	Pit	0	2	2	0
18	Stl	0	1	1	0
20	TB	1	0	1	0
23	Was	0	1	1	0
25	FLO	1	1	2	0
27	Buf	1	3	4	0
29	Fla	1	0	1	0
30	NJ	0	2	2	0
Nov 2	BOS	1	0	1	0
4	TB	0	1	1	0
6	NYI	0	0	0	0
9	WAS	0	1	1	0
11	Van	1	1	2	2
13	Phi	0	0	0	0
16	PIT	1	1	2	0
18	CAL	0	1	1	0
21	EDM	0	0	0	0
23	VAN	0	0	0	0
26	PHO	0	0	0	0
27	COL	0	1	1	0
Dec 1	Mon	0	1	1	0
4	Phi	0	1	1	0
6	Tor	2	2	4	0
7	TOR	1	0	1	0
9	Pho	0	3	3	0
11	Nyi	0	1	1	0
13	BUF	0	2	2	0
16	Har	1	1	2	2
18	La	0	3	3	0
21	MON	0	3	3	2
22	Fla	0	1	1	0
26	OTT	0	0	0	0
27	Ana	0	0	0	0
30	DAL	2	0	2	0
31	TB	0	0	0	0
Jan 2	Nyi	0	1	1	2
4	Ott	0	4	4	0
6	Col	0	0	0	2
8	Tb	0	1	1	0
9	WAS	0	0	0	0
12	Nj	0	2	2	0
13	Nyi	0	0	0	0
21	Edm	0	0	0	0
22	WAS	0	2	2	0
25	PIT	0	3	3	0
27	Chi	0	0	0	0
Feb 1	PHI	0	1	1	0
2	Bos	0	0	0	0
5	Har	0	4	4	2
8	NYI	0	1	1	0
9	FLO	0	1	1	0
13	STL	0	1	1	0
15	CHI	0	0	0	0
17	Nj	0	2	2	0
19	NJ	0	0	0	0
21	HAR	1	0	1	0
23	PHI	0	0	0	0
Mar 1	DET	0	0	0	10*
3	Sj	0	1	1	0
6	LA	1	1	2	0
7	ANA	0	1	1	0
9	SJ	0	2	2	2
12	Was	1	0	1	0
14	OTT	0	0	0	0
17	Ott	1	0	1	0
19	Mon	1	0	1	2
21	Det	1	0	1	0
24	Pit	1	1	2	0
27	NJ	0	0	0	0
29	HAR	0	1	1	0
Apr 1	Buf	0	0	0	0
3	Bos	1	0	1	0
4	BUF	1	0	1	0
7	Phi	0	2	2	0
10	PHI	0	2	2	0
11	Tb	0	0	0	0
TOTALS	82	25	72	97	28

* misconduct

1997–98 RANGERS

DATE	TEAM	G	A	P	Pim
Oct 3	Nyi	0	0	0	0
5	La	0	1	1	0
8	EDM	0	1	1	4
9	CAL	0	0	0	0
11	VAN	3	2	5	0
14	Pit	0	0	0	0
15	OTT	0	1	1	0
18	STL	0	1	1	0
20	Car	0	0	0	0
22	Chi	0	0	0	0
24	Tb	1	0	1	0
26	Ana	0	2	2	0
28	Dal	0	1	1	0
30	NYI	0	1	1	0
Nov 3	Edm	0	1	1	0
5	COL	1	2	3	0
7	DAL	1	0	1	0
12	Nj	0	1	1	0
14	Pit	0	0	0	0
16	Col	0	0	0	2
18	FLO	0	1	1	0
19	TB	0	1	1	0
21	CAR	1	2	3	0
22	PIT	0	0	0	0
25	Van	0	0	0	0
26	NYI	0	0	0	0
28	BUF	1	0	1	0
30	Fla	0	0	0	0
Dec 2	Was	1	0	1	0
5	Phi	0	1	1	0
6	MON	0	1	1	0
8	Pho	0	1	1	0
10	Cal	0	0	0	0
12	Fla	0	0	0	0
16	NJ	0	0	0	2
17	FLA	0	0	0	0
20	TB	0	1	1	0
21	Buf	0	0	0	0
23	Tb	0	3	3	0
26	BUF	0	0	0	0
28	Bos	1	1	2	0
31	TB	0	0	0	0
Jan 3	WAS	2	0	2	0
6	Car	0	2	2	2
8	Was	0	2	2	0
12	Tor	0	3	3	2
14	NJ	0	0	0	0
20	Stl	0	1	1	0
22	Phi	0	1	1	0
24	Nj	1	2	3	0
26	Was	0	1	1	0
29	OTT	0	1	1	0
31	BOS	0	1	1	0
Feb 2	SJ	0	1	1	0
4	ANA	0	1	1	0
5	LA	0	0	0	0
7	PHO	0	1	1	0
26	TOR	0	3	3	0
28	Phi	0	0	0	0
Mar 2	Buf	0	0	0	0
4	FLO	2	1	3	0
7	NJ	1	0	1	0
9	Nj	1	0	1	2
11	Sj	1	2	3	0
12	MON	0	0	0	0
14	BOS	0	1	1	0
16	Ott	0	4	4	0
18	Mon	0	1	1	0
21	Det	0	2	2	0
22	PHI	2	1	3	0
25	Ott	0	2	2	0
26	CAR	0	0	0	14*
28	PIT	0	1	1	0
30	Tb	0	1	1	0
Apr 1	Bos	1	0	1	0
4	NYI	0	0	0	0
5	CHI	0	1	1	0
7	Mon	1	1	2	0
11	DET	0	1	1	0
14	WAS	0	0	0	0
15	Nyi	1	1	2	0
18	PHI	0	1	1	0
TOTALS	82	23	67	90	28

* two minors/misconduct

1998–99 RANGERS

DATE	TEAM	G	A	P	Pim
Oct 9	Phi	0	0	0	0
10	MON	0	1	1	0
12	Stl	0	1	1	0
16	Nj	0	1	1	0
17	PIT	1	1	2	0
20	Edm	0	1	1	0
22	Nyi	0	0	0	0
24	PHI	0	1	1	0
27	Buf	0	0	0	0
30	Car	0	1	1	0
Nov 3	NJ	0	0	0	0
4	Mon	0	0	0	0
7	TOR	1	1	2	2
10	TB	0	2	2	0
11	FLO	0	1	1	0
13	Bos	0	2	2	0
18	ANA	0	1	1	2
19	LA	0	1	1	0
21	SJ	0	0	0	0
25	BUF	0	0	0	0
27	PIT	0	1	1	0
29	Nas	1	2	3	0
Dec 1	Flo	1	2	3	0
2	NYI	1	0	1	0
5	OTT	0	0	0	0
7	Tor	0	1	1	0
9	Col	0	1	1	0
11	BUF	0	0	0	2
14	Cal	0	3	3	0
16	NJ	1	2	3	0
19	TOR	0	2	2	0
23	Car	0	0	0	0
26	CAR	0	0	0	0
30	PHO	0	0	0	0
31	COL	0	2	2	0
Jan 2	STL	0	0	0	0

DATE	TEAM	G	A	P	Pim
4	Sj	0	1	1	0
6	Nj	0	0	0	0
7	WAS	0	0	0	0
10	Tb	1	1	2	0
13	Nyi	0	2	2	0
15	Chi	0	0	0	0
16	MON	0	0	0	0
19	Ott	0	1	1	0
21	Flo	0	0	0	0
26	WAS	0	3	3	0
28	CAR	0	0	0	0
30	DET	0	1	1	0
Feb 1	Was	0	0	0	0
4	Van	1	2	3	0
7	BOS	0	0	0	0
12	Car	0	0	0	2
14	Det	0	0	0	0
15	NAS	0	5	5	0
17	Mon	0	0	0	0
19	Pit	0	1	1	0
21	EDM	0	0	0	0
22	CAL	0	1	1	0
26	Pho	did not play			
28	Phi	did not play			
Mar 2	Dal	did not play			
4	WAS	did not play			
7	BOS	did not play			
8	Tor	did not play			
10	Ott	did not play			
12	Bos	did not play			
14	NYI	did not play			
15	Was	did not play			
19	Buf	did not play			
21	Pit	did not play			
22	TB	0	0	0	0
24	FLO	0	0	0	2
27	PHI	0	0	0	0
29	Nyi	1	0	1	0
Apr 2	Ana	0	0	0	4
4	NJ	0	0	0	0
5	PHI	0	2	2	0
8	CHI	0	0	0	0
9	DAL	0	0	0	0
12	Tb	0	1	1	0
15	OTT	0	0	0	0
18	Pit	0	1	1	0
TOTALS 70		9	53	62	14

PLAYOFFS

1980 EDMONTON

DATE	TEAM	G	A	P	Pim
Apr 8	PHI	1	1	2	0
9	PHI	0	0	0	0
11	Phi	1	0	1	0
TOTALS 3		2	1	3	0

1981 EDMONTON

DATE	TEAM	G	A	P	Pim
Apr 8	MON	0	5	5	2
9	MON	0	2	2	0
11	Mon	3	1	4	0
16	NYI	1	0	1	0
17	NYI	0	1	1	2
19	Nyi	3	0	3	0
20	Nyi	0	2	2	0

DATE	TEAM	G	A	P	Pim
22	NYI	0	2	2	0
24	Nyi	0	1	1	0
TOTALS 9		7	14	21	4

1982 EDMONTON

DATE	TEAM	G	A	P	Pim
Apr 7	La	1	3	4	4
8	La	1	1	2	2
10	LA	2	2	4	2
12	LA	0	1	1	0
13	La	1	0	1	0
TOTALS 5		5	7	12	8

1983 EDMONTON

DATE	TEAM	G	A	P	Pim
Apr 6	Win	4	1	5	0
7	Win	0	2	2	0
9	WIN	0	1	1	0
14	Cal	0	0	0	0
15	Cal	0	2	2	2
17	CAL	4	3	7	0
18	CAL	1	1	2	0
20	Cal	1	2	3	0
24	Chi	1	4	5	0
26	Chi	0	2	2	0
May 1	CHI	0	2	2	2
3	CHI	1	2	3	0
10	Nyi	0	0	0	0
12	Nyi	0	2	2	0
14	NYI	0	1	1	0
17	NYI	0	1	1	0
TOTALS 16		12	26	38	4

1984 EDMONTON

DATE	TEAM	G	A	P	Pim
Apr 4	Win	0	3	3	0
5	Win	1	1	2	0
7	WIN	0	0	0	2
12	Cal	2	2	4	0
13	Cal	1	1	2	0
15	CAL	0	1	1	0
16	CAL	0	1	1	2
18	Cal	0	0	0	0
20	CAL	0	2	2	0
22	Cal	1	2	3	0
24	Min	1	3	4	2
26	Min	1	1	2	0
28	MIN	2	1	3	2
May 1	MIN	0	1	1	0
10	NYI	0	0	0	0
12	NYI	0	0	0	2
15	Nyi	0	2	2	0
17	Nyi	2	0	2	2
19	Nyi	2	1	3	0
TOTALS 19		13	22	35	12

1985 EDMONTON

DATE	TEAM	G	A	P	Pim
Apr 10	La	0	2	2	2
11	La	0	1	1	0
13	LA	0	2	2	0
18	Win	1	2	3	0
20	Win	1	0	1	0

DATE	TEAM	G	A	P	Pim
23	WIN	1	1	2	0
25	WIN	3	4	7	0
May 4	Chi	1	3	4	0
7	Chi	0	3	3	0
9	CHI	0	0	0	0
12	CHI	1	2	3	2
14	Chi	2	2	4	0
16	CHI	0	4	4	0
21	PHI	0	0	0	0
23	PHI	1	0	1	0
25	Phi	3	1	4	0
28	Phi	2	0	2	0
30	Phi	1	3	4	0
TOTALS 18		17	30	47	4

1986 EDMONTON

DATE	TEAM	G	A	P	Pim
Apr 9	Van	1	0	1	0
10	Van	1	1	2	0
12	VAN	1	2	3	2
18	Cal	0	1	1	0
20	Cal	0	1	1	0
22	CAL	1	1	2	0
24	CAL	3	2	5	0
26	Cal	1	0	1	0
28	CAL	0	2	2	0
30	Cal	0	1	1	0
TOTALS 10		8	11	19	2

1987 EDMONTON

DATE	TEAM	G	A	P	Pim
Apr 8	La	0	1	1	0
9	La	1	6	7	0
11	LA	0	2	2	0
12	LA	1	4	5	0
14	La	0	0	0	0
21	Win	0	0	0	0
23	Win	0	2	2	0
25	WIN	0	3	3	0
27	WIN	1	0	1	0
May 5	Det	0	0	0	0
7	Det	0	1	1	0
9	DET	0	0	0	0
11	DET	0	1	1	2
13	Det	0	0	0	2
17	Phi	1	1	2	0
20	Phi	1	1	2	0
22	PHI	0	1	1	0
24	PHI	0	3	3	2
26	Phi	0	1	1	0
28	PHI	0	1	1	0
31	Phi	0	1	1	0
TOTALS 21		5	29	34	6

1988 EDMONTON

DATE	TEAM	G	A	P	Pim
Apr 6	Win	0	2	2	0
7	Win	0	0	0	2
9	WIN	0	1	1	0
10	WIN	0	3	3	0
12	Win	1	4	5	2
19	CAL	1	0	1	2
21	CAL	2	0	2	0
23	Cal	0	2	2	0
25	Cal	1	0	1	0

DATE	TEAM	G	A	P	Pim
May 3	Det	0	3	3	0
5	Det	1	2	3	0
7	DET	2	0	2	10*
9	DET	0	2	2	0
11	Det	1	2	3	0
18	Bos	1	0	1	0
20	Bos	1	2	3	0
22	BOS	0	4	4	0
24	BOS	0	2	2	0**
26	Bos	1	2	3	0
TOTALS 19		12	31	43	16

* misconduct
** game cancelled but statistics count

1989 LOS ANGELES

DATE	TEAM	G	A	P	Pim
Apr 5	Edm	0	1	1	0
6	Edm	1	1	2	0
8	EDM	0	0	0	0
9	EDM	0	3	3	0
11	Edm	1	2	3	0
13	EDM	0	1	1	0
15	Edm	2	1	3	0
18	CAL	0	2	2	0
20	CAL	0	3	3	0
22	Cal	0	1	1	0
24	Cal	1	2	3	0
TOTALS 11		5	17	22	0

1990 LOS ANGELES

DATE	TEAM	G	A	P	Pim
Apr 4	CAL	did not play			
6	CAL	did not play			
8	Cal	0	1	1	0
10	Cal	1	4	5	0
12	CAL	0	0	0	0
14	Cal	1	2	3	0
18	EDM	0	0	0	0
20	EDM	0	0	0	0
22	Edm	1	0	1	0
24	Edm	did not play			
TOTALS 7		3	7	10	0

1991 LOS ANGELES

DATE	TEAM	G	A	P	Pim
Apr 4	Van	1	1	2	0
6	Van	1	0	1	0
8	VAN	1	0	1	0
10	VAN	1	1	2	0
12	Van	0	4	4	0
14	VAN	0	0	0	0
18	Edm	0	2	2	0
20	Edm	0	0	0	0
22	EDM	0	0	0	0
24	EDM	0	2	2	0
26	Edm	0	0	0	2
28	EDM	0	1	1	0
TOTALS 12		4	11	15	2

1992 LOS ANGELES

DATE	TEAM	G	A	P	Pim
Apr 18	Edm	0	0	0	0

DATE	TEAM	G	A	P	Pim
20	Edm	0	4	4	2
22	EDM	0	0	0	0
24	EDM	0	1	1	0
26	Edm	2	0	2	0
28	EDM	0	0	0	0
TOTALS	6	2	5	7	2

1993 LOS ANGELES

DATE	TEAM	G	A	P	Pim
Apr 18	CAL	0	1	1	0
21	CAL	0	1	1	0
23	Cal	0	1	1	0
25	Cal	0	0	0	2
27	CAL	1	3	4	0
29	Cal	1	2	3	0
May 2	VAN	1	0	1	0
5	VAN	1	2	3	0
7	Van	2	1	3	0
9	Van	0	2	2	0
11	VAN	1	0	1	0
13	Van	1	2	3	0
17	TOR	0	1	1	0
19	TOR	0	1	1	0
21	Tor	0	1	1	0
23	Tor	1	1	2	0
25	TOR	0	0	0	0
27	Tor	1	0	1	0
29	TOR	3	1	4	0
Jun 1	MON	1	3	4	2
3	MON	0	0	0	0
5	Mon	1	1	2	0
7	Mon	0	1	1	0
9	MON	0	0	0	0
TOTALS	24	15	25	40	4

1994 LOS ANGELES

DID NOT QUALIFY

1995 LOS ANGELES

DID NOT QUALIFY

1996 ST. LOUIS

DATE	TEAM	G	A	P	Pim
Apr 16	TOR	0	3	3	0
18	TOR	0	1	1	0
21	Tor	0	1	1	0
23	Tor	0	3	3	0
25	TOR	0	1	1	0
27	Tor	0	0	0	0
May 3	DET	0	1	1	0
5	DET	0	1	1	0
8	Det	0	1	1	0
10	Det	1	0	1	0
12	DET	1	1	2	0
14	Det	0	1	1	0
16	DET	0	0	0	0
TOTALS	13	2	14	16	0

1997 RANGERS

DATE	TEAM	G	A	P	Pim
Apr 17	FLO	0	0	0	0
20	FLO	1	1	2	0
22	Flo	0	1	1	0
23	Flo	3	0	3	0
25	FLO	0	0	0	2
May 2	NJ	0	0	0	0
4	NJ	0	1	1	0
6	Nj	1	1	2	0
8	Nj	1	0	1	0
11	NJ	0	1	1	0
16	PHI	0	1	1	0
18	PHI	3	0	3	0
20	Phi	1	1	2	0
23	Phi	0	1	1	0
25	PHI	0	2	2	0
TOTALS	15	10	10	20	2

1998 RANGERS

DID NOT QUALIFY

1999 RANGERS

DID NOT QUALIFY

INTERNATIONAL GAMES

1978 WORLD JUNIOR CHAMPIONSHIPS

DATE	OPPONENT	G	A	P	Pim
Dec 22/77	vs. United States	1	1	2	0
Dec 23/77	vs. West Germany	3	2	5	0
Dec 25/77	vs. Czechoslovakia	3	3	6	0
Dec 28/77	vs. Soviet Union	0	0	0	0
Dec 31/77	vs. Czechoslovakia	1	0	1	2
Jan 1/78	vs. Sweden	0	3	3	0
TOTALS	6 GAMES	8	9	17	2

1979 WHA ALL-STARS/MOSCOW DYNAMO

DATE	OPPONENT	G	A	P	Pim
Jan 2/79	vs. Dynamo	2	1	3	0
Jan 4/79	vs. Dynamo	1	1	2	0
Jan 5/79	vs. Dynamo	0	0	0	0
TOTALS	3 GAMES	3	2	5	0

1981 CANADA CUP

DATE	OPPONENT	G	A	P	Pim
Sept 1/81	vs. Finland	2	1	3	0
Sept 3/81	vs. United States	2	2	4	0
Sept 5/81	vs. Czechoslovakia	0	0	0	0
Sept 7/81	vs. Sweden	0	1	1	0
Sept 9/81	vs. Soviet Union	1	2	3	0
Sept 11/81	vs. United States	0	1	1	2
Sept 13/81	vs. Soviet Union	0	0	0	0
TOTALS	7 GAMES	5	7	12	2

1982 WORLD CHAMPIONSHIPS

DATE	OPPONENT	G	A	P	Pim
Apr 15/82	vs. Finland	0	1	1	0
Apr 16/82	vs. Czechoslovakia	0	0	0	0
Apr 18/82	vs. Sweden	0	0	0	0
Apr 19/82	vs. West Germany	0	2	2	0
Apr 21/82	vs. Italy	0	0	0	0
Apr 22/82	vs. United States	2	1	3	0
Apr 24/82	vs. Soviet Union	0	1	1	0
Apr 25/82	vs. Soviet Union	1	0	1	0
Apr 27/82	vs. Czechoslovakia	0	1	1	0
Apr 29/82	vs. Sweden	3	2	5	0
TOTALS	10 GAMES	6	8	14	0

1984 CANADA CUP

DATE	OPPONENT	G	A	P	Pim
Sept 1/84	vs. West Germany	3	1	4	0
Sept 3/84	vs. United States	0	0	0	2
Sept 6/84	vs. Sweden	0	0	0	0
Sept 8/84	vs. Czechoslovakia	0	1	1	0
Sept 10/84	vs. Soviet Union	0	2	2	0
Sept 13/84	vs. Soviet Union	0	1	1	0
Sept 16/84	vs. Sweden	1	2	3	0
Sept 18/84	vs. Sweden	1	0	1	0
TOTALS	8 GAMES	5	7	12	2

1987 RENDEZ-VOUS

DATE	OPPONENT	G	A	P	Pim
Feb 11/87	vs. Soviet Union	0	1	1	0
Feb 13/87	vs. Soviet Union	0	3	3	0
TOTALS	2 GAMES	0	4	4	0

1987 CANADA CUP

DATE	OPPONENT	G	A	P	Pim
Aug 28/87	vs. Czechoslovakia	0	2	2	0
Aug 30/87	vs. Finland	0	0	0	0
Sept 2/87	vs. United States	0	2	2	0
Sept 4/87	vs. Sweden	1	3	4	2
Sept 6/87	vs. Soviet Union	1	1	2	0
Sept 8/87	vs. Czechoslovakia	0	2	2	0
Sept 11/87	vs. Soviet Union	1	1	2	0
Sept 13/87	vs. Soviet Union	0	5	5	0
Sept 15/87	vs. Soviet Union	0	2	2	0
TOTALS	9 GAMES	3	18	21	2

1991 CANADA CUP

DATE	OPPONENT	G	A	P	Pim
Aug 31/91	vs. Finland	0	0	0	2
Sept 2/91	vs. United States	1	3	4	0
Sept 5/91	vs. Sweden	0	3	3	0
Sept 7/91	vs. Czechoslovakia	2	1	3	0
Sept 9/91	vs. Soviet Union	0	0	0	0
Sept 12/91	vs. Sweden	1	0	1	0
Sept 14/91	vs. United States	0	1	1	0
Sept 16/91	vs. United States	did not play			
TOTALS	7 GAMES	4	8	12	2

1996 WORLD CUP

DATE	OPPONENT	G	A	P	Pim
Aug 28/96	vs. Russia	0	2	2	0
Aug 31/96	vs. United States	2	0	2	2
Sept 1/96	vs. Slovakia	0	0	0	0
Sept 5/96	vs. Germany	1	0	1	0
Sept 7/96	vs. Sweden	0	0	0	0
Sept 10/96	vs. United States	0	0	0	0
Sept 12/96	vs. United States	0	0	0	0
Sept 14/96	vs. United States	0	1	1	0
TOTALS	8 GAMES	3	3	6	2

1998 OLYMPIC WINTER GAMES

DATE	OPPONENT	G	A	P	Pim
Feb 13/98	vs. Belarus	0	0	0	0
Feb 14/98	vs. Sweden	0	0	0	0
Feb 16/98	vs. United States	0	1	1	2
Feb 18/98	vs. Kazakhstan	0	2	2	0
Feb 20/98	vs. Czech Republic	0	0	0	0
Feb 21/98	vs. Finland	0	1	1	0
TOTALS	6 GAMES	0	4	4	2

ACKNOWLEDGEMENTS

THE AUTHOR WOULD LIKE TO THANK the many people who helped out with information, time, expertise, and support in getting the book done faster than pronto. First, to the wonderful group at the Hockey Hall of Fame, namely Phil Pritchard (who, like Wayne, is well on his way to fathering a hockey team of his own), Craig "climb-the-highest-mountain-for-you" Campbell, Jane Rodney, Darren Boyko, Jacqueline Boughazale, Tracey Green, Sophie Harding, Marilyn Robbins, and Izak Westgate. To Kathy Webster, Ed Arnold, Francine Bellefeuille, Anne-Marie Beaton and Andrea Gordon, John Haluka, Jefferson Davis and Peggy Mackenzie. To the Great One of the agenting world, Dean Cooke, and his forbearing assistants, Suzanne Brandreth and Scott Colbourne. To everyone at Doubleday who got the Gretzky show on the road, notably editor and word-genius Christine Innes, Janine Laporte, Belinda Kemp, Brad Martin, John Pearce, and John Neale. To Jon Redfern, Geri Dasgupta, and Jack David, for one thing and another, namely support. And to my mom, C.M., for letting me watch *Hockey Night in Canada* every Saturday night when I was just nothin' but a kid.

PHOTO CREDITS

Bruce Bennett Studios: front cover, back cover, pages 6, 23, 29, 31, 33, 34, 39, 41, 43, 44, 46, 47, 53, 54, 60, 65, 67, 68, 69, 71, 72–3, 80, 81, 83, 84, 87, 88, 89, 91, 95, 96, 97, 98, 99, 100, 101, 104, 105, 107, 110, 113, 114, 116, 117, 122, 125, 126, 129, 135, 136

Canapress: pages 8, 22, 45, 48, 55, 56, 57, 58, 59, 61, 62, 63, 66, 75, 79, 93, 94, 113, 115, 123, 127, 128, 132, 139, 140, 141

David Sandford/Hockey Hall of Fame: title page, pages 109, 121, 130–31, 133, 137

Doug MacLellan/Hockey Hall of Fame: pages 82, 108, 118, 124

London Life–Portnoy/Hockey Hall of Fame: pages 24, 25, 35, 36, 37

Graphic Artists/Hockey Hall of Fame: page 18

Miles Nadal/Hockey Hall of Fame: pages 70, 74

Phoenix Roadrunners/Hockey Hall of Fame: page 111

John Rea/Hockey Hall of Fame: page 9

Hockey Hall of Fame Archives: pages 10, 12, 17, 20, 30, 32, 143

Sports Action/Steve Babineau: pages 19, 21, 42, 77, 86

Sports Action/Brian Babineau: page 123

Sports Action/Lee Calkins: page 112

Jack Dobson/*Globe and Mail*: page 26

Edward Regan/*Globe and Mail*: page 119

Dennis Robinson/*Globe and Mail*: pages 5, 7

Thomas Szlukovenyi/*Globe and Mail*: page 49

Jeffrey Goode/*Toronto Star*: page 50

***The Sault Star*:** pages 14, 15

***Peterborough Examiner*:** page 11

John Sokolowski: page 102

ALSO BY ANDREW PODNIEKS

Hello Hockey Fans: The Hockey Book of Lists (with Jefferson Davis, 1999)

Red, White, and Gold: Canada at the World Junior Championships 1974–1999 (1998)

*Shooting Stars: Photographs from the Portnoy Collection at the
Hockey Hall of Fame* (1998)

*Portraits of the Game: Classic Photographs from the Turofsky Collection
at the Hockey Hall of Fame* (1997)

Canada's Olympic Hockey Teams: The Complete History: 1920–1998 (1997)

*The Blue and White Book 1997: The Most Complete
Toronto Maple Leafs Fact Book Ever Published* (1996)

*The Red Wings Books: The Most Complete Detroit Red Wings
Fact Book Ever Published* (1996)

*The Blue and White Book: The Most Complete Toronto Maple Leafs
Fact Book Ever Published* (1995)

Return to Glory: The Leafs From Imlach to Fletcher (1995)

For Children

Hockey Heroes: Paul Kariya (2000)

Hockey Heroes: Patrick Roy (1998)